Creativity and the Writing Process

Creativity and
the Writing Process

Edited by

Olivia Bertagnolli
Jeff Rackham
University of North Carolina

1807 1982

175 YEARS OF PUBLISHING

John Wiley & Sons
New York   Chichester   Brisbane   Toronto   Singapore

Library of Congress Cataloging in Publication Data
Main entry under title:

Creativity and the writing process.

   1. Creative writing. 2. Creation (Literary,
artistic, etc.)   I. Bertagnolli, Olivia.   II. Rackham, Jeff.
PN145.c88   808'.042   81-18671
ISBN 0-471-08806-4   AACR2

Printed in the United States of America

10 9 8 7 6 5 4 3 2 1

Preface

The writing process often seems inexplicable. It is at once internal, complex, indefinable, individual, and organic. Yet those who have struggled with writing, those who have wrestled with the blank page and felt the fear of failure, who ultimately in unexpected moments have found themselves breaking through, *can* offer insights into the creative process. The authors selected for this collection speak from personal human experience; they make writing seem possible rather than formidable. Collectively and individually they urge those of us interested in writing to begin with memory and emotion, to freely explore and play with language, to see and internalize what is seen, to trust the intuitive voice, and to combine self-discipline with patience. Most of all, they express the belief that in pursuing writing as a creative process, writers enrich their own lives as human beings.

Experienced teachers and writers will recognize a number of these essays. Those by Maslow, Rilke, Engle, and Spender are now considered classic statements on how the imagination works. We have included them here because, especially for the beginning writer, they retain their force and clarity. Other essays represent the work of major contemporary authors, including William Stafford, Richard Hugo, Denise Levertov, Marvin Bell, and Joyce Carol Oates. Many of these have appeared only within the last ten years and reflect insights gained by younger authors still engaged in the creative struggle. Two new essays, those by David Huddle and Glenn Jackson, are published here for the first time. Our attempt has been to blend classic with contemporary and to offer new writers a broad range of ideas and insights on how the writing process works. With only a few exceptions we have limited our selections to those who speak of their own personal efforts. We have eliminated several important studies that deal in theoretical aspects of creativity, such as Carl Sagan's *Dragons of Eden*. For those who wish to pursue the subject, however, such works have been included in the Suggested Readings.

Stephen Spender's essay, "The Making of a Poem," has provided us with the organization for this anthology. Spender was one of the first modern poets to attempt a description of how the creative process worked for him; and his categories—Concentration, Inspiration, Memory, Faith, and Song—still seem useful. We have added a prefatory grouping of essays under the general title, The Creative Process, and included Spender's own piece there. And we have added a concluding category—Technique—in which three authors including Flannery O'Connor, discuss the relationship between technique and process. We believe that this structure, from the general overview of creativity, through the various stages of the intuitive process, toward more conscious working with technique and craft, provides a movement similar to the organic process itself, one that should allow the essays to be read productively in sequence. For the student or teacher who wishes to be more selective, the categories and quotations in the Contents should allow one to choose the essay a new writer might need at any one phase of development. It remains clear, of course, that when dealing with creativity, all of these divisions serve for convenience only. The mysterious process that occurs inside artists as they work cannot be categorized or defined. Consequently, the following collection does not place limits on the subject of creativity. Instead, it provides a selection of voices that we hope will encourage new writers to more freely explore the uniqueness of their own creative process.

OLIVIA BERTAGNOLLI

JEFF RACKHAM

Contents

. . . the creative person . . . loses his past and his future and lives only in the moment. He is all there, totally immersed, fascinated and . . . "utterly lost in the present."

It is a characteristic of our time that many people are afraid of solitude: to be alone is a sign one is a social failure . . . [yet] if we are to experience insights from our unconscious, we need to be able to give ourselves to solitude.

Inspiration is the beginning of a poem and also its final goal. . . . In between this start and this winning post there is the hard race, the sweat and toil.

Forget all rules, forget all restrictions, as to taste, as to what ought to be said, write for the pleasure of it—whether slowly or fast—every form of resistance to a complete release should be abandoned.

I tell you that I have a long way to go before I am where one begins. . . .

You are so young, so before all·beginning, and I want to beg you, as much as I can, to be patient toward all that is unsolved in your heart and to try to love the questions themselves *like locked rooms and like books that are written in a very foreign tongue. Do not now seek the answers, which cannot be given you because you would not be able to live them. And the point is, to live everything. Live the questions now. Perhaps you will then gradually, without noticing it, live along some distant day into the answer.*

Resolve to be always beginning—to be a beginner!

Rainer Maria Rilke at age 45

Introduction

The best writers have seldom written only to publish. Through hard work and continual effort, they have learned there is joy in the *act* of writing, a pleasure in discovering who and what they are as human beings and what it means to be alive. If the pleasure of the act results in a published product, fine. It feels good to know that someone, even a single editor, likes what you have written. But most writers who have published will admit the real satisfaction comes in the writing. It is the process, not the product, that validates their lives.

The product is the end result of a process. It is the finished painting hanging above a fireplace, the completed story, the poem or novel typed in final form and stashed away in a drawer. Whether written quickly and spontaneously or worked at over a period of years, when we are satisfied (at least for the time being) that there is nothing more to add or delete, no changes to be made, nothing more to do with those specific images and emotions, we have before us, for better or worse, the *product* of our labor. We are ready to begin another poem, another story.

For the beginning writer, however, focusing on the product may be misleading and even inhibiting. This is especially true when we compare our own products with those of well-known authors. The poems and stories we read by Yeats or Chekhov represent only a select portion of those writers' actual work. What we see in print may be the result of a lifetime struggle. What we don't see are the false starts, the endless drafts, the failures. Theodore Roethke's notebooks fill twelve horizontal feet of library shelves in the University of Washington Manuscript Collection. Only seven volumes have been abstracted from fifteen-thousand-page transcripts of the original diaries writ-

1

ten by Anaïs Nin. Poet William Stafford admits that only one out of ten poems he sends to publishers is ever printed. At seventeen, intent on being published, Sylvia Plath received forty-five rejection slips from *Seventeen* magazine before a short story was finally accepted. Writers and editors glean what they judge to be the best. (They've been known to make mistakes: Emily Dickinson had only seven poems published during her lifetime although she wrote over 1,700.)

Yet as beginning writers we often expect instant results. We want what we write to equal what we've just read, focusing on the final product alone, forgetting all the years of hard work that may have preceded it. When our attempts don't measure up, we feel frustrated. All too often we forget to begin where we are, to accept what we write as our own, to forget the product and commit ourselves to the process itself.

But what *is* the process? Admittedly, anyone who attempts to probe that mystery may end up with more questions than answers. According to Kenneth Burke, "Even if we had a record of every . . . single step involved in the actual writing of a poem, of the exact order in which revisions were made, of the author's dreams and personal quandaries during the writing, of his borrowings from other authors or from situations in life itself . . . even if we had a mountain of such data, we should have but a fraction of the information needed to chart fully that work's genesis."

Yet if we can't be sure of the process, we can be sure of what it is not. It is not an orderly set of rules and regulations which, if practiced diligently, will turn us into writers. That in itself is important for the beginning writer to know. Confronted by a choice of writing programs, workshops, and conferences, the new writer may be misled into believing writing is an art that can be acquired—a matter of attending classes, fulfilling assignments. Ads in popular magazines promise to turn us into writers in a matter of months. We often talk about techniques, craft, structure, the dialogue between characters. We learn to identify the frame tale, iambic pentameter, hyperboles, and oxymorons. There is nothing wrong with this except that literary criticism—which is the point of issue here—should not be confused with writing. They are not the same. Certainly, the more we learn about our craft, the better, but the beginning writer must be reminded that learning to write is mostly a matter of continuous work to be accomplished alone.

In most instances, the development of a poem or story from the point of inspiration, through the initial rendering of the images in words on paper, and the final development from the primitive form to the finished, polished product, demands work and patience extended quite often over a significant period of time. We know that experiences and emotions stored away in our unconscious need time to gestate. We know that the constant struggle to express concretely what is felt intuitively usually necessitates hours of solitude, hours of work. For many of us the act of writing is one way of discovering what is hidden inside us, a way of gaining access to the imagination, to memory, to emotions. In this sense we know we cannot separate writing from living, from being alive, from the life we have lived. The process we are talking about then is an "organic" one, what Thomas Huxley considered "almost an equivalent of the word 'living'." The world we experience and our perceptions of it, what we taste and smell and see, what we feel with our fingertips, the sounds we hear, are the raw material of our stories and poems. Consciously and unconsciously, we are gleaners and gatherers, foraging images, storing them in our unconscious until we allow our imaginations to recover them.

Analogies between the process of writing and the process of painting are not uncommon. Our own understanding of creative process may be clarified by American artist Georgia O'Keeffe's journal description of her particular process written after she had worked on a series of paintings titled Shell and Old Shingle. As writers collect experiences, artists collect objects. Georgia O'Keeffe gathers bones, rocks, pieces of wood—all subjects of her paintings. Once, rather absentmindedly, she recalls, she picked up an old barn shingle and took it home where she placed it next to a clam shell. A few days later she noticed the shell against the shingle and began painting. She painted what she saw: the literal shingle and shell. Dissatisfied with the results, she painted the shingle and shell over and over, much as a writer might move through several drafts or revisions. But in each painting the shell remained a shell, the shingle a shingle; nothing emerged with any sense of spirit. Being the true artist, O'Keeffe didn't give up. After painting the shingle and shell a fourth time, she sensed herself moving beyond the literal subject and painted instead the imagined one. This time the shingle became a dark space floating above a white space. "The shapes," she writes, "seemed to sing." Months later, O'Keeffe painted a misty landscape of a mountain outside her window and realized sometime afterward that the mountain in the painting had taken on the shape of the shingle on the table. She had allowed the literal shingle and shell to become fictionalized by her imagination. Her early attempts to capture the literal material, conscious and controlled attempts, failed to satisfy her. The final painting was an uncontrolled, spontaneous act, the result of allowing the experience to incubate, and of having the patience and trust to allow the imagination to discover for itself the mountain in the shape of a shingle. A similar process happens to most artists—painters or writers—although never in quite the same way, even for the same person. The process cannot be hurried or forced or willed, but when the fictionalized memories of our experiences surface, when the image begins to sing, we must be ready.

In the same way that O'Keeffe began by painting the literal shell and shingle, beginning writers sometimes attempt to write about literal experiences. The death of a loved one, a trip back home after a long absence, an experience in a local bar, three crows in a locust tree—all may seem like good material for a story or a poem, and may be, but usually when we attempt to write about an experience too soon, we are overpowered by the literal elements. We end up reporting the actual event and feel frustrated that our writing fails to take off on its own. We discover and reveal nothing new because the images are still consciously controlled. Experience must be understood as constituting only the raw material of our writing. Like wine stored in oak casks, experience must be stored away in the unconscious where it will begin the slow, rich process of fermentation and aging, changing from the literal to the imagined—a process that may take months or years. Rainer Maria Rilke began the *Duino Elegies* in 1912 but was unable to finish the poem until ten years later when he completed the work within a single month of intense effort.

This early phase of the process often requires another condition—what Virginia Woolf pleaded for in *A Room of One's Own*—a place where one can think and write in solitude. It was Rilke who admitted that "works of art are of infinite loneliness." In solitude we dream and feel. In solitude we allow our imaginations to work for us. Promising everything and nothing, the imagination cannot be forced into activity, yet if we are patient and willing to wait without feeling guilt or self-condemnation for those seemingly wasted hours, we may recover those images and emotions that make writing possible. In a letter to his brother Theo, Vincent Van Gogh wrote, "one cannot do right away what one wants. It will come gradually . . . in art one cannot have too much patience." Poet Richard Hugo finds his solitude while trout fishing on the shores of a lake in Montana. Thoreau walked the woods. Wallace Stevens spent hours looking at pictures in a museum of some New England town. Whether walking or staring out a window, it is this period of solitude that re-awakens the senses and allows those images stored away in the subconscious to surface if they are ready. What may appear idle, wasted time to others is a necessary condition preceding and promoting the creative process. In solitude we give passionate attention to our lives, to our memories, to the details around us. In solitude we return to fish the dark pond of the imagination. Eventually most writers learn to accept solitude as a necessary condition, trusting that during those quiet periods when nothing at all seems to be happening, the unconscious is actively sorting, organizing, and fusing images.

Still it is actual writing—the practice and habit of writing—that exercises our receptivity and teaches us to accept, for better or worse, what the imagination gives. When an emotion triggers an image, the individual already engaged in writing is ready to follow it. Almost all writers profit from writing every day. Many have kept personal journals, a place where they feel free to relax and drift, to write anything whatever. Ann Morrow Lindbergh, Joan Didion, May Sarton, Sylvia Plath, Dylan Thomas, Mark Twain, Andre Gide, Somerset Maugham, Theodore Roethke are only a few. Writing freely and spontaneously, in addition to loosening the ligaments, is one way of lubricating the unconscious, easing the flow of words to paper. Very often what begins as a journal entry re-surfaces months or years later in some fictionalized form. Reflecting upon a year's journal, Virginia Woolf noted, "if I stopped and thought, it would never be written at all; and the advantage of the method is that it sweeps up accidentally several stray matters which I should exclude if I hesitated, but which are the diamonds of the dustheap."

Writing generates writing. The act of writing stirs up images, emotions, memories. We're often surprised, stimulated by our discoveries. What is exciting about the creative process is that we don't know where our imagination will lead us.

Many times an image that suddenly carries us off in one direction may lead nowhere. This is not unusual. In fact, we're misled more often than not. All writers learn to accept these temporary failures as a necessary part of the creative process. It's a hard lesson to learn, but as Eudora Welty once observed, "No art ever came out of not risking your neck. And risk—experimentation—is a considerable part of the joy of doing." What is necessary for the beginning writer is to have faith and confidence in the imagination, to write simply and freely from the heart without concern for failure or success.

And then sometimes when we're writing freely, drifting along, accepting anything that comes to mind, we feel a sudden agitation, an excitement. Michelangelo believed the statues he sculpted were already hidden inside the marble. He could not quite visualize the figure, but he knew it was only a matter of chipping away the surface. Writers have this feeling too: they don't know where the image is leading them, but they know it's guiding them toward something important. John Fowles describes how he was haunted for five months by the image of a young woman standing at the end of a small pier. Again and again the image returned, inexplicable and mysterious. For Fowles, she was a figure hidden in the marble.

Such a feeling might be referred to as inspiration but if that's what it is, it comes as a result of hard work. The time spent daydreaming, the continued effort to write spontaneously day after day, the willingness to accept small failures and yet continue, prepares us, cultivates our receptivity to the triggering image or emotion that leads to what psychologist Abraham Maslow describes as "peak experience." This slightly heady inebriation of the heart is the reason most writers write. The working out of the idea may come in a single burst and seem to complete itself within minutes or hours. Other times the process is much slower. Even after five months, Fowles did not know who the woman in his image was, or what story she had to tell. He wrote 140,000 words before he had a satisfactory rough draft and then took more than another year of polishing before *The French Lieutenant's Woman* was complete. In the same manner, the triggering image for Richard Wilbur's poem, "The Eye," came to him a year and a half before he began to write about it; even then the poem took a number of months to finish. And Marvin Bell admits that drafts of his poems sometimes sit for years before he feels they are ready for submission. By contrast, Eudora Welty tells how she wrote the entire short story, "Powerhouse," in a single evening after attending a concert.

Inspiration probably begins with writing that is basically intuitive and may then shift back and forth in some mysterious way between conscious and unconscious. E. L. Doctorow has described how he always finds himself in the midst of such chaos. "Sometimes," he says, "I can't go on until a page is perfect. Other times I go on for 50 pages or 100 pages and throw the whole thing out and start over. In *Daniel* I wrote 150 pages of straight chronological narrative and threw them all away in great despair. It wasn't until I did that that I very recklessly sat down and began the book the way it should have begun." Writing as an organic process then seems to take on a life of its own, leading us on an adventure over which we have little control. The more fully conscious aspect of writing, the crafting and revising, usually comes much later, when we work at condensing, editing, and polishing. Yet even then, writing is never merely a matter of mastering technique or craft. We would do well to remember James Wright's advice to simplify the language and enlarge the heart—the source of our best and most lasting work.

Anyone who attempts to categorize or define these various aspects of the writing process risks failure. After all is said and done, we are left with an oversimplification of a complex phenomenon that seems to defy explanation. Nevertheless, as beginning writers, if we are serious about our work, we cannot remain ignorant of process or we risk far greater failure. An awareness of process, if nothing else, may relieve feelings of guilt and self-condemnation; it may help us overcome the notion that writing is easier for others; it may lead us to accept the necessary frustrations that serious writers learn to tolerate. However, these are the least important justifications. The movement away from writing that is product-oriented and the movement toward writing as process engaged in for the reward of discovering images, memories, and emotions, is an act of self-acceptance. It may in some quiet, unforeseen way, promote a work of art that is well worth waiting a lifetime for. Again and again in reading the following essays by experienced writers who so generously share their own inner processes with us, we hear Rilke's voice saying, "Do not look outward . . . go into yourself. Seek the depths of things. Seek the depths of things."

The Creative Process

If you want to draw a bird, you must become a bird.

Hokusai

I looked out the window and saw a sparrow and I became the sparrow. I saw a piece of straw and I became the straw.

Keats

Abraham Maslow was one of America's most eminent psychologists and authors noted for his pioneering work in humanist psychology. Originally a follower of Freud, he broke with Freud for, among other things, his belief that creativity was not a way of releasing one's neurotic inhibitions, but instead one of the highest expressions of human well-being. At Brandeis University Maslow was Philip Meyers Professor of Psychology and Chairman of the Psychology department from 1951 to 1961. At the time of his death in 1961, he was investigating the nature of evil in man. Among his most well-known works are *Motivation and Personality* (1956), *Toward Psychology of Science* (1965), and *The Farther Reaches of Human Nature* (1971) from which "The Creative Attitude" is excerpted.

The Creative Attitude

Abraham H. Maslow

We're pretty clearly aware now from our psychological analysis of the process of creativeness and of creative individuals, that we must make the distinction between primary creativeness and a secondary creativeness. The primary creativeness or the inspirational phase of creativeness must be separated from the working out and the development of the inspiration. This is because the latter phase stresses not only creativeness, but also relies very much on just plain hard work, on the discipline of the artist who may spend half a life time learning his tools, his skills, and his materials, until he becomes finally ready for a full expression of what he sees. I am very certain that many, many people have waked up in the middle of the night with a flash of inspiration about some novel they would like to write, or a play or a poem or whatever and that most of these inspirations never came to anything. Inspirations are a dime a dozen. The difference between the inspiration and the final product, for example, Tolstoy's *War and Peace,* is an awful lot of hard work, an awful lot of discipline, an awful lot of training, an awful lot of finger exercises and practices and rehearsals and throwing away first drafts and so on.

Source: *From* The Farther Reaches of Human Nature *by Abraham Maslow. Copyright* © 1971 by *Bertha G. Maslow. Reprinted by permission of Viking Penguin Inc.*

The puzzle that I'm now trying to unravel is suggested by the observation that the creative person, in the inspirational phase of the creative furor, loses his past and his future and lives only in the moment. He is all there, totally immersed, fascinated and absorbed in the present, in the current situation, in the here-now, with the matter-in-hand. Or to use a perfect phrase from *The Spinster* by Sylvia Ashton-Warner, the teacher absorbed with a new method of teaching reading to her children says, "I am utterly lost in the present."

This ability to become "lost in the present" seems to be a *sine qua non* for creativeness of any kind. But also certain *prerequisites* of creativeness—in whatever realm—somehow have something to do with this ability to become timeless, selfless, outside of space, of society, of history.

It has begun to appear strongly that this phenomenon is a diluted, more secular, more frequent version of the mystical experience that has been described so often as to have become what Huxley called *The Perennial Philosophy*. In various cultures and in various eras, it takes on somewhat different coloration—and yet its essence is always recognizable—it is the same.

It is always described as a loss of self or of ego, or sometimes as a transcendence of self. There is a fusion with the reality being observed (with the matter-in-hand, I shall say more neutrally), a oneness where there was a twoness, an integration of some sort of the self with the non-self. There is universally reported a seeing of formerly hidden truth, a revelation in the strict sense, a stripping away of veils, and finally, almost always, the whole experience is experienced as bliss, ecstasy, rapture, exaltation.

Little wonder that this shaking experience has so often been considered to be superhuman, supernatural, so much greater and grander than anything conceivable as human that it could only be attributed to trans-human sources. And such "revelations" often serve as basis, sometimes the *sole* basis, for the various "revealed" religions.

And yet even this most remarkable of all experiences has now been brought into the realm of human experience and cognition. My researches on what I call peak experiences and Marghanita Laski's on what she calls ecstasies done quite independently of each other, show that these experiences are quite naturalistic, quite easily investigated and, what is to the point right now, that they have much to teach us about creativeness as well as other aspects of the full functioning of human beings when they are most fully realizing themselves, most mature and evolved, most healthy, when, in a word, they are most fully human.

One main characteristic of the peak experience is just this total fascination with the matter-in-hand, this getting lost in the present, this detachment from time and place. And it seems to me now that much of what we have learned from the study of these peak experiences can be transferred quite directly to the enriched understanding of the here-now experience, of the creative attitude.

It is not necessary for us to confine ourselves to these uncommon and rather extreme experiences, even though it now seems clear that practically all people can report moments of rapture if they dig around long enough in their memories, and if the interview situation is just right. We can also refer to the simplest version of the peak experience, namely fascination, concentration, or absorption in *anything* which is interesting enough to hold this attention completely. And I mean not only great symphonies or tragedies; the job can be done by a gripping movie or detective story, or simply becoming absorbed with one's work. There are certain advantages in starting from such universal and familiar experiences which we all have, so that we can get a direct feeling or intuition or empathy, that is, a direct experiential knowledge of a modest, moderate, version of the fancier "high" experiences. For one thing we can avoid the flossy, high-flying, extremely metaphorical vocabulary that is so common in this realm.

Well then, what are some of the things that happen in these moments?

GIVING UP THE PAST

The best way to view a present problem is to give it all you've got, to study *it* and its nature, to perceive *within* it the intrinsic interrelationships, to discover (rather than to invent) the answer to the problem within the problem itself. This is also the best way to look at a painting or to listen to a patient in therapy.

The other way is merely a matter of shuffling over past experiences, past habits, past knowledge to find out in what respects this current situation is similar to some situation in the past, i.e., to classify it, and then to use *now* the solution that once worked for the similar problem in the past. This can be likened to the work of a filing clerk. I have called it "rubricizing." And it works well enough to the extent that the present *is* like the past.

But obviously it *doesn't* work in so far as the matter-in-hand is different from the past. The file-clerk approach fails then. This person confronting an unknown painting hurriedly runs back through his knowledge of art history to remember how he is supposed to react. Meanwhile of course he is hardly looking at the painting. All he needs is the name or the style or the content to enable him to do his quick calculations. He then enjoys it if he is supposed to, and doesn't if he is *not* supposed to.

In such a person, the past is an inert, undigested foreign body which the person carries about. It is not yet the person himself.

More accurately said: The past is active and alive only insofar as it has re-created the person, and has been digested into the present person. It is not or should not be something *other* than the person, something alien to it. It has now become Person (and has lost its own identity as something different and other), just as past steaks that I have eaten are now me, *not* steaks. The digested past (assimilated by intussusception) is different from the undigested past. It is Lewin's "ahistorical past."

GIVING UP THE FUTURE

Often we use the present not for its own sake but in order to prepare for the future. Think how often in a conversation we put on a listening face as the other person talks, secretly however preparing what we are going to say, rehearsing, planning a counterattack perhaps. Think how different your attitude would be right now if you knew you were to comment on my remarks in five minutes. Think how hard it would be then to be a good, total listener.

If we are totally listening or totally looking, we have thereby given up this kind of "preparing for the future." We don't treat the present as merely a means to some future end (thereby devaluating the present). And obviously, this kind of forgetting the future is a prerequisite to total involvement with the present. Just as obviously, a good way to "forget" the future is not to be apprehensive about it.

Of course, this is only one sense of the concept "future." The future which is within us, part of our present selves, is another story altogether.

INNOCENCE

This amounts to a kind of "innocence" of perceiving and behaving. Something of the sort has often been attributed to highly creative people. They are variously described as being naked in the situation, guileless, without *a priori* expectations, without "shoulds" or "oughts," without fashions, fads, dogmas, habits, or other pictures-in-the-head of what is proper, normal, "right," as being ready to receive whatever happens to be the case without surprise, shock, indignation, or denial.

Children are more able to be receptive in this undemanding way. So are wise old people. And it appears now that we *all* may be more innocent in this style when we become "here-now."

NARROWING OF CONSCIOUSNESS

We have now become much less conscious of everything other than the matter-in-hand (less distractible). *Very* important here is our lessened awareness of other people, of their ties to us and ours to them, of obligations, duties, fears, hopes, etc. We become much more free of other people, which in turn, means that we become much more ourselves, our Real Selves (Horney), our authentic selves, our real identity.

This is so because *the* greatest cause of our alienation from our real selves is our neurotic involvements with other people, the historical hangovers from childhood, the irrational transferences, in which past and present are confused, and in which the adult acts like a child. (By the way, it's all right for the *child* to act like a child. His dependencies on other people can be very real. *But,* after all, he *is* supposed to outgrow them. To be afraid of what daddy will say or do is certainly out of place if daddy has been dead for twenty years.)

In a word, we become more free of the influence of other people in such moments. So, insofar as these influences have affected our behavior, they no longer do so.

This means dropping masks, dropping our efforts to influence, to impress, to please, to be lovable, to win applause. It could be said so: If we have no audience to play to, we cease to be actors. With no need to act we can devote ourselves, self-forgetfully, to the problem.

LOSS OF EGO: SELF-FORGETFULNESS, LOSS OF SELF-CONSCIOUSNESS

When you are totally absorbed in non-self, you tend to become less conscious of yourself, less self-aware. You are less apt to be observing yourself like a spectator or a critic. To use the language of psychodynamics, you become less dissociated than usual into a self-observing ego and an experiencing ego; i.e., you come much closer to being *all* experiencing ego. (You tend to lose the shyness and bashfulness of the adolescent, the painful awareness of being looked at, etc.). This in turn means more unifying, more oneness and integration of the person.

It also means less criticizing and editing, less evaluating, less selecting and rejecting, less judging and weighing, less splitting and analyzing of the experience.

This kind of self-forgetfulness is one of the paths to finding one's true identity, one's real self, one's authentic nature, one's deepest nature. It is almost always felt as pleasant and desirable. We needn't go so far as the Buddhists and Eastern thinkers do in talking about the "accursed ego"; and yet there *is* something in what they say.

INHIBITING FORCE OF CONSCIOUSNESS (OF SELF)

In some senses consciousness (especially of self) is inhibiting in some ways and at some times. It is sometimes the locus of doubts, conflicts, fears, etc. It is sometimes harmful to full-functioning creativeness. It is sometimes an inhibitor of spontaneity and of expressiveness (*but* the observing ego is necessary for therapy).

And yet it is also true that some kind of self-awareness, self-observation, self-criticism—i.e., the self-observing ego—*is* necessary for "secondary creativeness." To use psychotherapy as an example, the task of self-improvement is partly a consequence of criticizing the experiences that one has allowed to come into consciousness. Schizophrenic people experience many insights and yet don't make therapeutic use of them because they are too much "totally experiencing" and not enough "self-observing-and-criticizing." In creative work, likewise, the labor of disciplined construction succeeds upon the phase of "inspiration."

FEARS DISAPPEAR

This means that our fears and anxieties also tend to disappear. So also our depressions, conflicts, ambivalence, our worries, our problems, even our physical pains. Even—for the moment—our psychoses and our neuroses (that is, if they are not so extreme as to prevent us from becoming deeply interested and immersed in the matter-in-hand).

For the time being, we are courageous and confident, unafraid, unanxious, unneurotic, not sick.

LESSENING OF DEFENSES AND INHIBITIONS

Our inhibitions also tend to disappear. So also our guardedness, our (Freudian) defenses, and controls (brakes) on our impulses as well as the defenses against danger and threat.

STRENGTH AND COURAGE

The creative attitude requires both courage and strength and most studies of creative people have reported one or another version of courage: stubbornness, independence, self-sufficiency, a kind of arrogance, strength of character, ego-strength, etc.; popularity becomes a minor consideration. Fear and weakness cast out creativeness or at least make it less likely.

It seems to me that this aspect of creativeness becomes somewhat more understandable when it is seen as a part of the syndrome of here-now self-forgetfulness and other-forgetfulness. Such a state intrinsically implies less fear, less inhibition, less need for defense and self-protection, less guardedness, less need for artificiality, less fear of ridicule, of humiliation and of failure. All these characteristics are *part of* self-forgetfulness and audience-forgetfulness. Absorption casts out fear.

Or we can say in a more positive way, that becoming more courageous makes it easier to let oneself be attracted by mystery, by the unfamiliar, by the novel, by the ambiguous and contradictory, by the unusual and unexpected, etc., instead of becoming suspicious, fearful, guarded, or having to throw into action our anxiety-allaying mechanisms and defenses.

ACCEPTANCE: THE POSITIVE ATTITUDE

In moments of here-now immersion and self-forgetfulness we are apt to become more "positive" and less negative in still another way, namely, in giving up criticism (editing, picking and choosing, correcting, skepticism, improving, doubting, rejecting, judging, evaluating). This is like saying that we accept. We don't reject or disapprove or selectively pick and choose.

No blocks against the matter-in-hand means that we let it flow in upon us. We let it wreak its will upon us. We let it have its way. We let it be itself. Perhaps we can even approve of its being itself.

This makes it easier to be Taoistic in the sense of humility, noninterference, receptivity.

TRUST VS. TRYING, CONTROLLING, STRIVING

All of the foregoing happenings imply a kind of trust in the self and a trust in the world which permits the temporary giving up of straining and striving, of volition and control, of conscious coping and effort. To permit oneself to be determined by the intrinsic nature of the matter-in-hand here-now necessarily implies relaxation, waiting, receiving. The common effort to master, to dominate, and to control are antithetical to a true coming-to-terms with or a true perceiving of the materials (or the problem, or the person, etc.). Especially is this true with respect to the future. We *must* trust our ability to improvise when confronted with novelty in the future. Phrased in this way, we can see more clearly that trust involves self-confidence, courage, lack of fear of the world. It is also clear that this kind of trust in ourselves-facing-the-unknown-future is a condition of being able to turn totally, nakedly, and wholeheartedly to the present.

FULLEST SPONTANEITY

If we are fully concentrated on the matter-in-hand, fascinated with it for its own sake, having no other goals or purposes in mind, then it is easier to be fully spontaneous, fully functioning, letting our capacities flow forth easily from within, of themselves, without effort, without conscious volition or control, in an instinct-like, automatic, thoughtless way; i.e., the fullest, least obstructed, most organized action.

The one main determinant of their organization and adaptation to the matter-in-hand is then most apt to be the intrinsic nature of the matter-in-hand. Our capacities then adapt to the situation most perfectly, quickly, effortlessly, and change flexibly as the situation changes; e.g., a painter continuously adapts himself to the demands of his developing painting; as a wrestler adapts himself to his opponent; as a pair of fine dancers mutually adapt to each other; as water flows into cracks and contours.

FULLEST EXPRESSIVENESS (OF UNIQUENESS)

Full spontaneity is a guarantee of honest expression of the nature and the style of the freely functioning organism, and of its uniqueness. Both words, spontaneity and expressiveness, imply honesty, naturalness, truthfulness, lack of guile, nonimitativeness, etc., because they also imply a noninstrumental nature of the behavior, a lack of willful "trying," a lack of effortful striving or straining, a lack of interference with the flow of the impulses and the free "radiating" expression of the deep person.

The only determinants now are the intrinsic nature of the matter-in-hand, the intrinsic nature of the person and the intrinsic necessities of their fluctuating adaptation to each other to form a fusion, a unit; e.g., a fine basketball team, or a string quartet. Nothing outside this fusion situation is relevant. The situation is not a means to any extrinsic end; it is an end in itself.

FUSION OF THE PERSON WITH THE WORLD

We wind up with the fusion between the person and his world which has so often been reported as an observable fact in creativeness, and which we may now reasonably consider to be a *sine qua non*. I think that this spider web of interrelationships that I have been teasing apart and discussing can help us to understand this fusion better as a natural event, rather than as something mysterious, arcane, esoteric. I think it can be researched if we understand it to be an isomorphism, a molding of each to each other, a better and better fitting together or complementarity, a melting into one.

It has helped me to understand what Hokusai meant when he said, "If you want to draw a bird, you must become a bird."

Rollo May   earned his B.A. in English from Oberlin College, a Bachelor of Divinity from Union Theological Seminary in New York, and then practiced ministry two years before he enrolled in Columbia University to study clinical psychology. During the early 1930s, he contracted tuberculosis and was given a fifty-fifty chance of survival. "I learned quickly to tune in on my being, my existence in the *now*," he has recalled. As an existential psychotherapist and humanist, May believes that human beings must be made aware of and responsible for their own lives. Motivational force, he argues, must come from within, without regard for the expectations and approval of others. May's books include *The Meaning of Anxiety: Man's Search for Himself* (1952), *Psychology and the Human Dilemma* (1966), *Love and Will* (1969), *Power and Innocence: A Search for the Sources of Violence* (1962), and *The Courage to Create* (1975) from which the following essay is excerpted. May spends most of his summers on a fifty-acre farm in Holderness, New Hampshire, writing, painting (mostly watercolors), and tending birches.

Creativity and the Unconscious

Rollo May

Everyone uses from time to time such expressions as, "a thought pops up," an idea comes "from the blue" or "dawns" or "comes as though out of a dream," or "it suddenly hit me." These are various ways of describing a common experience: the breakthrough of ideas from some depth below the level of awareness. I shall call this realm "the unconscious" as a catchall for the subconscious, preconscious, and other dimensions below awareness.

When I use the phrase "the unconscious," I, of course, mean it as a shorthand. There is no such thing as *"the* unconscious"; it is, rather, unconscious dimensions (or aspects or sources) of experience. I define this unconscious as *the potentialities for awareness or action which the individual cannot or will not actualize.* These potentialities are the source of what can be called "free creativity." The exploration of unconscious phenomena has a fascinating relationship to creativity. What are the nature and characteristics of the creativity that has its source in these unconscious depths of personality?

Source: *Selection is reprinted from* The Courage to Create *by Rollo May, with the permission of W. W. Norton & Company, Inc. Copyright © 1975 by Rollo May.*

I wish to begin our exploration of this topic by relating an incident from my own experience. When I was a graduate student doing research on *The Meaning of Anxiety*, I studied anxiety in a group of unmarried mothers—i.e., pregnant young women in their late teens and early twenties in a shelter home in New York City. I had a good, sound hypothesis on anxiety, approved by my professors and approved by me—that the predisposition toward anxiety in individuals would be proportionate to the degree to which they had been rejected by their mothers. In psychoanalysis and psychology this had been a generally accepted hypothesis. I assumed the anxiety of people like these young women would be cued off by the anxiety-creating situation of being unwed and pregnant, and I could then study more openly the original source of their anxiety—namely the maternal rejection.

Now I discovered that half the young women fitted my hypothesis beautifully. But the other half did not fit it at all. This latter group included young women from Harlem and the Lower East Side who had been radically rejected by their mothers. One of them, whom I shall call Helen, was from a family of twelve children whose mother drove them out of the house on the first day of summer to stay with their father, the caretaker of a barge that went up and down the Hudson River. Helen was pregnant by her father. At the time she was in the shelter, he was in Sing Sing on a charge of rape by Helen's older sister. Like the other young women of this group, Helen would say to me, "We have troubles, but we don't worry."

This was a very curious thing to me and I had a hard time believing the data. But the facts seemed clear. As far as I could tell by the Rorschach, TAT, and other tests I used, these radically rejected young women did not carry any unusual degree of anxiety. Forced out of the house by their mothers, they simply made their friends among other youngsters on the street. Hence, there was not the predisposition to anxiety we would have expected according to what we know in psychology.

How could this be? Had the rejected young women who had not experienced anxiety become hardened, apathetic, so that they did not feel the rejection? The answer to that seemed clearly no. Were they psychopathic or sociopathic types, who also don't experience anxiety? Again, no. I felt myself caught by an insoluble problem.

Late one day, putting aside my books and papers in the little office I used in that shelter house, I walked down the street toward the subway. I was tired. I tried to put the whole troublesome business out of my mind. About fifty feet away from the entrance to the Eighth Street station, it suddenly struck me "out of the blue," as the not-unfitting expression goes, that those young women who didn't fit my hypothesis *were all from the proletarian class*. And as quickly as that idea struck me, other ideas poured out. I think I had not taken another step on the sidewalk when a whole new hypothesis broke loose in my mind. I realized my entire theory would have to be changed. I saw at that instant that it is not rejection by the mother that is the original trauma which is the source of anxiety; it is rather *rejection that is lied about*.

The proletarian mothers rejected their children, but they never made any bones about it. The children knew they were rejected; they went out on the streets and found other companions. There was never any subterfuge about their situation. They knew their world—bad or good—and they could orient themselves to it. But the middle class young women were always lied to in their families. They were rejected by mothers who pretended they loved them. This was really the source of their anxiety, not the sheer rejection. I saw, in that instantaneous way that characterizes insights from these deeper sources, that anxiety comes from *not being able to know the world you're in, not being able to orient yourself in your own existence.* I was convinced there, on the street—and later thought and experience only convinced me the more—that this is a better, more accurate, and more elegant theory, than my first.

What was going on at the moment when this breakthrough occurred? Taking this experience of mine as a start, we notice, first of all, that the insight broke into my conscious mind *against* what I had been trying to think rationally. I had a good, sound thesis and I had been working very hard trying to prove it. The unconscious, so to speak, *broke through in opposition to the conscious belief to which I was clinging.*

Carl Jung often made the point that there is a polarity, a kind of opposition, between unconscious experience and consciousness. He believed the relationship was compensatory: consciousness controls the wild, illogical vagaries of the unconscious, while the unconscious keeps consciousness from drying up in banal, empty, arid rationality. The compensation also works on specific problems: if I consciously bend too far one way on some issue, my unconscious will lean the other way. This is, of course, the reason why the more we are unconsciously smitten with doubts about an idea, the more dogmatically we fight for it in our conscious arguments. This is also why persons as different as Saint Paul on the Damascus road and the alcoholic in the Bowery go through such radical conversions—the repressed unconscious side of the dialectic erupts and takes over the personality. The unconscious seems to take delight (if I may so express it) in breaking through—and breaking up—exactly what we cling to most rigidly in our conscious thinking.

What occurs in this breakthrough is not simply growth; it is much more dynamic. It is not a mere expansion of awareness; it is rather a kind of battle. A dynamic struggle goes on within a person between what he or she consciously thinks on the one hand and, on the other, some insight, some perspective that is struggling to be born. The insight is then born with anxiety, guilt, and the joy and gratification that is inseparable from the actualizing of a new idea or vision.

The guilt that is present when this breakthrough occurs has its source in the fact that the insight must destroy something. My insight destroyed my other hypothesis and would destroy what a number of my professors believed, a fact that caused me some concern. Whenever there is a breakthrough of a significant idea in science or a significant new form in art, the new idea will destroy what a lot of people believe is essential to the survival of their intellectual and spiritual world. This is the source of guilt in genuine creative work. As Picasso remarked, "Every act of creation is first of all an act of destruction."

The breakthrough carries with it also an element of anxiety. For it not only broke down my previous hypothesis, it shook my self-world relationship. At such a time I find myself having to seek a new foundation, the existence of which I as yet don't know. This is the source of the anxious feeling that comes at the moment of the breakthrough; it is not possible that there be a genuinely new idea without this shake up occurring to some degree.

But beyond guilt and anxiety, as I said above, the main feeling that comes with the breakthrough is one of gratification. We have seen something new. We have the joy of participating in what the physicists and other natural scientists call an experience of "elegance."

A second thing that occurred in the breakthrough of this insight is that *everything around me became suddenly vivid.* I can remember that on the particular street down which I walked the houses were painted an ugly shade of green that I normally would prefer to forget immediately. But by virtue of the vividness of this experience, the colors all around were sharpened and were imbedded in my experience, and that ugly green still exists in my memory. The moment the insight broke through, there was a special translucence that enveloped the world, and my vision was given a special clarity. I am convinced that this is the usual accompaniment of the breakthrough of unconscious experience into consciousness. Here is again part of the reason the experience scares us so much: the world, both inwardly and outwardly, takes on an intensity that may be momentarily overwhelming. This is one aspect of what is called ecstasy—the uniting of unconscious experience with consciousness, a union that is not *in abstracto,* but a dynamic, immediate fusion.

I want to emphasize that I did not get my insight as though I were dreaming, with the world and myself opaque and cloudy. It is a popular misconception that perception is dull when one is experiencing this state of insight. I believe that perception is actually sharper. True, one aspect of it resembles a dream in that self and world may become kaleidoscopic; but another aspect of the experience is a sharpened perception, a vividness, a translucence of relationship to the things around us. The world becomes vivid and unforgettable. Thus the breakthrough of material from unconscious dimensions involves a heightening of sensory experience.

We could, indeed, define the whole experience that we are talking about as *a state of heightened consciousness.* Unconsciousness is the depth dimension of consciousness, and when it surges up into consciousness in this kind of polar struggle the result is an intensification of consciousness. It heightenes not only the capacity to think, but also the sensory processes; and it certainly intensifies memory.

There is a third thing we observe when such insights occur—that is, *the insight never comes hit or miss, but in accordance with a pattern of which one essential element is our own commitment.* The breakthrough does not come by just "taking it easy," by "letting the unconscious do it." The insight, rather, is born from unconscious levels exactly in the areas in which we are most intensively consciously committed. The insight came to me on that problem to which, up till the moment I put my books and papers away in the little office that I occupied, I had devoted my best and most energetic conscious thought. The idea, the new form which suddenly becomes present, *came in order to complete an incomplete Gestalt with which I was struggling in conscious awareness.* One can quite accurately speak of this incomplete Gestalt, this unfinished pattern, this unformed form, as constituting the "call" that was answered by the unconscious.

The fourth characteristic of this experience is that *the insight comes at a moment of transition between work and relaxation.* It comes at a break in periods of voluntary effort. My breakthrough came when I had put away my books and was walking toward the subway, my mind far away from that problem. It is as though intense application to the problem—thinking about it, struggling with it—starts and keeps the work process going; but some part of the pattern that is different from what I am trying to work out is struggling to be born. Hence the tension that is involved in creative activity. If we are too rigid, dogmatic, or bound to previous conclusions, we will, of course, never let this new element come into our consciousness; we will never let ourselves be aware of the knowledge that exists on another level within us. But the insight often cannot be born until the conscious tension, the conscious application, is relaxed. Hence the well-known phenomenon that the unconscious breakthrough requires the alternation of intense, conscious work and relaxation, with the unconscious insight often occurring, as in my case, at the moment of the shift.

Albert Einstein once asked a friend of mine in Princeton, "Why is it I get my best ideas in the morning while I'm shaving?" My friend answered, as I have been trying to say here, that often the mind needs the relaxation of inner controls—needs to be freed in reverie or day dreaming—for the unaccustomed ideas to emerge.

Let us now consider the experience, more complex and richer than mine, of one of the great mathematicians of the late nineteenth and early twentieth centuries, Jules Henri Poincaré. In his autobiography, Poincaré tells us with admirable clarity how his new insights and new theories came to him, and he describes vividly the circumstances surrounding the occurrence of one "breakthrough."

> *For fifteen days I strove to prove that there could not be any functions like those I have since called Fuchsian functions. I was then very ignorant; every day I seated myself at my work table, stayed an hour or two, tried a great number of combinations and reached no results. One evening, contrary to my custom, I drank black coffee and could not sleep. Ideas rose in crowds; I felt them collide until pairs interlocked, so to speak, making a stable combination. By the next morning I had established the existence of a class of Fuchsian functions, those which come from the hypergeometric series; I had only to write out the results, which took but a few hours.*

Still a young man, he was then called into the military service, and for some months nothing happened in his thinking. One day in a town in southern France he was getting on a bus and talking with another soldier. As he was about to put his foot on the step—he pinpoints the moment that exactly—there broke into his mind the answer to how these new mathematical functions that he had discovered were related to the conventional mathematics he had been working on before. When I read Poincaré's experience—which was after the above incident in my own life—I was struck by how similar it was in this special precision and vividness. He got up on the step, entered the bus, continued without pause his conversation with his friend, but was completely and instantaneously convinced of the way these functions were related to general mathematics.

To continue with a later portion of his autobiography, when he returned from army service:

> *Then I turned my attention to the study of some arithmetical questions apparently without much success and without a suspicion of any connection with my preceding researches. Disgusted with my failure, I went to spend a few days at the seaside, and thought of something else. One morning, walking on the bluff, the idea came to me, with just the same characteristics of brevity, suddenness and immediate certainty, that the arithmetic transformations of indeterminate ternary quadratic forms were identical with those of non-Euclidean geometry.*

Poincaré, turning psychologist for the moment, asks himself the question we posed above: What is going on in the mind that these ideas should break through at this moment? This is what he proposes in answer to his question:

> *Most striking at first is this appearance of sudden illumination, a manifest sign of long, unconscious prior work. The role of this unconscious work in mathematical invention appears to me incontestable, and traces of it would be found in other cases where it is less evident. Often when one works at a hard*

question, nothing good is accomplished at the first attack. Then one takes a rest, longer or shorter, and sits down anew to the work. During the first half-hour, as before, nothing is found, and then all of a sudden the decisive idea presents itself to the mind. It might be said that the conscious work has been more fruitful because it has been interrupted and the rest has given back to the mind its force and freshness.

Is the appearance of the illumination due to the relief from fatigue—i.e., simply taking a rest? No, he answers:

It is more probable that this rest has been filled out with unconscious work and that the result of this work has afterward revealed itself to the geometer just as in the cases I have cited; only the revelation, instead of coming during a walk or a journey, has happened during a period of conscious work, but independently of this work which plays at most a role of excitant, as if it were the goad stimulating the results already reached during rest, but remaining unconscious, to assume the conscious form.

He then continues with another penetrating comment on the practical aspects of the breakthrough:

There is another remark to be made about the conditions of this unconscious work: it is possible, and of a certainty it is only fruitful, if it is on the one hand preceded and on the other hand followed by a period of conscious work. These sudden inspirations (and the examples already cited sufficiently prove this) never happen except after some days of voluntary effort which has appeared absolutely fruitless and whence nothing good seems to have come, where the way taken seems totally astray. These efforts then have not been as sterile as one thinks; they have set agoing the unconscious machine and without them it would not have moved and would have produced nothing.

Let us summarize some of the most significant points so far in Poincaré's testimony. He sees the characteristics of the experience as follows: (1) the *suddenness* of the illumination; (2) that the insight may occur, and to some extent *must* occur, *against* what one has clung to consciously in one's theories; (3) the *vividness* of the incident and the whole scene that surrounds it; (4) the *brevity* and *consciseness* of the insight, along with the experience of *immediate certainty*. Continuing with the practical conditions which he cites as necessary for this experience are (5) hard work on the topic *prior to the breakthrough*; (6) a *rest*, in which the "unconscious work" has been given a chance to proceed on its own and after which the breakthrough may occur (which is a special case of the more general point); (7) the necessity of *alternating work and relaxation*, with the insight often coming at the moment of the break between the two, or at least within the break.

This last point is particularly interesting. It is probably something everyone has learned: professors will lecture with more inspiration if they occasionally alternate the classroom with the beach; authors will write better when, as Macaulay used to do, they write for two hours, then pitch quoits, and then go back to their writing. But certainly more than the mere mechanical alternation is involved.

I propose that in our day this alternation of the market place and mountain requires the capacity for the *constructive use of solitude*. It requires that we be able to retire from a world that is "too much with us," that we be able to be quiet, that we let the solitude work for us and in us. It is a characteristic of our time that many people are afraid of solitude: to be alone is a sign one is a social failure, for no one would be alone if he or she could help it. It often occurs to me that people living in our modern, hectic civilization, amid the constant din of radio and TV, subjecting themselves to every kind of stimulation whether of the passive sort of TV or the more active sort of conversation, work, and activity, that people with such constant preoccupations find it exceedingly difficult to let insights from unconscious depths break through. Of course, when an individual is afraid of the irrational—that is, of the unconscious dimensions of experience—he tries to keep busiest, tries to keep most "noise" going on about him. The avoidance of the anxiety of solitude by constant agitated diversion is what Kierkegaard, in a nice simile, likened to the settlers in the early days of America who used to beat on pots and pans at night to make enough din to keep the wolves away. Obviously if we are to experience insights from our unconscious, we need to be able to give ourselves to solitude.

Poincaré finally asks: What determines *why* a given idea comes through from the unconscious? Why this particular insight and not one of a dozen others? Is it because a particular insight is the answer which is empirically most accurate? No, he answers. Is it because it is the insight which will pragmatically work best? Again, no. What Poincaré proposes as the selective factor resulting in this given insight seems to me to be in some ways the most important and gripping point in his whole analysis:

> The useful combinations [that come through from the unconscious] are precisely the most beautiful, I mean those best able to charm this special sensibility that all mathematicians know, but of which the profane are so ignorant as often to be tempted to smile at it.
>
> ... Among the great numbers of combinations blindly formed by the subliminal self, almost all are without interest and without utility; but just for that reason they are also without effect upon the esthetic sensibility. Consciousness will never know them; only certain ones are harmonious, and, consequently, at once useful and beautiful. They will be capable of touching this special sensibility of the geometer of which I have just spoken, and which, once aroused, will call our attention to them, and thus give them occasion to become conscious.

This is why the mathematicians and physicists talk about the "elegance" of a theory. The utility is subsumed as part of the character of being beautiful.

The harmony of an internal form, the inner consistency of a theory, the character of beauty that touches one's sensibilities—these are significant factors determining why a given idea emerges. As a psychoanalyst, I can only add that my experience in helping people achieve insights reveals the same phenomenon—that insights emerge not chiefly because they are "rationally true" or even helpful, but because they have a certain form, the form that is beautiful because it completes an incomplete Gestalt.

When this breakthrough of a creative insight into consciousness occurs, we have the subjective conviction that the form should be this way and no other way. It is characteristic of the creative experience that it strikes us as true—with the "immediate certainty" of Poincaré. And we think, nothing else could have been true in that situation, and we wonder why we were so stupid as not to have seen it earlier. The reason, of course, is that we were not psychologically ready to see it. We could not yet *intend* the new truth or creative form in art or scientific theory. We were not yet open on the level of intentionality. But the "truth" itself is simply there. This reminds us of what the Zen Buddhists keep saying—that at these moments is reflected and revealed a reality of the universe that does not depend merely on our own subjectivity, but is as though we only had our eyes closed and suddenly we open them and there it is, as simple as can be. The new reality has a kind of immutable, eternal quality. The experience that "this is the way reality is and isn't it strange we didn't see it sooner" may have a religious quality with artists. This is why many artists feel that something holy is going on when they paint, that there is something in the act of creating which is like a religious revelation.

Stephen Spender, British poet, essayist, and journalist, was one of the original group of Oxford Poets who revolutionized English verse in the 1930s. In his long lifetime he has written, edited, or contributed to more than 75 volumes of poetry, fiction, essays, drama, and biography, including *The Creative Element* (1953), a study of the creative process at work in major authors of the twentieth century. His last collection of poems, *The Generous Days* (1971), contains work written, and in some cases rewritten, over the past two decades. "The Making of a Poem" is now considered one of the classic essays on creativity in the arts.

The Making of a Poem

Stephen Spender

CONCENTRATION

The problem of creative writing is essentially one of concentration, and the supposed eccentricities of poets are usually due to mechanical habits or rituals developed in order to concentrate. Concentration, of course, for the purposes of writing poetry, is different from the kind of concentration required for working out a sum. It is a focusing of the attention in a special way, so that the poet is aware of all the implications and possible developments of his idea, just as one might say that a plant was not concentrating on developing mechanically in one direction, but in many directions, towards the warmth and light with its leaves, and towards the water with its roots, all at the same time.

Schiller liked to have a smell of rotten apples, concealed beneath the lid of his desk, under his nose when he was composing poetry. Walter de la Mare has told me that he must smoke when writing. Auden drinks endless cups of tea. Coffee is my own addiction, besides smoking a great deal, which I hardly ever do except when I am writing. I notice also that as I attain a greater concentration, this tends to make me forget the taste of the cigarette in my mouth, and then I have a desire to smoke two or even three cigarettes at a

Source: *Reprinted by permission of A D Peters & Co Ltd.*

time, in order that the sensation from the outside may penetrate through the wall of concentration which I have built round myself.

For goodness' sake, though, do not think that rotten apples or cigarettes or tea have anything to do with the quality of the work of a Schiller, a de la Mare, or an Auden. They are a part of a concentration which has already been attained rather than the causes of concentration. De la Mare once said to me that he thought the desire to smoke when writing poetry arose from a need, not of a stimulus, but to canalize a disturbing leak of his attention away from his writing towards the distraction which is always present in one's environment. Concentration may be disturbed by someone whistling in the street or the ticking of a clock. There is always a slight tendency of the body to sabotage the attention of the mind by providing some distraction. If this need for distraction can be directed into one channel—such as the odour of rotten apples or the taste of tobacco or tea—then other distractions outside oneself are put out of competition.

Another possible explanation is that the concentrated effort of writing poetry is a spiritual activity which makes one completely forget, for the time being, that one has a body. It is a disturbance of the balance of body and mind and for this reason one needs a kind of anchor of sensation with the physical world. Hence the craving for a scent or taste or even, sometimes, for sexual activity. Poets speak of the necessity of writing poetry rather than of a liking for doing it. It is spiritual compulsion, a straining of the mind to attain heights surrounded by abysses and it cannot be entirely happy, for, in the most important sense, the only reward worth having is absolutely denied: for, however confident a poet may be, he is never quite sure that all his energy is not misdirected nor that what he is writing is great poetry. At the moment when art achieves its highest attainment it reaches beyond its medium of words or paints or music, and the artist finds himself realizing that these instruments are inadequate to the spirit of what he is trying to say.

Different poets concentrate in different ways. In my own mind I make a sharp distinction between two types of concentration: one is immediate and complete, the other is plodding and only completed by stages. Some poets write immediately works which, when they are written, scarcely need revision. Others write their poems by stages, feeling their way from rough draft to rough draft, until finally, after many revisions, they have produced a result which may seem to have very little connection with their early sketches.

These two opposite processes are vividly illustrated in two examples drawn from music: Mozart and Beethoven. Mozart thought out symphonies, quartets, even scenes from operas, entirely in his head—often on a journey or perhaps while dealing with pressing problems—and then he transcribed them, in their completeness, on to paper. Beethoven wrote fragments of themes in notebooks which he kept beside him, working on and developing them over years. Often his first ideas were of a clumsiness which makes scholars marvel how he could, at the end, have developed from them such miraculous results.

Thus genius works in different ways to achieve its ends. But although the Mozartian type of genius is the more brilliant and dazzling, genius, unlike virtuosity, is judged by greatness of results, not by brilliance of performance. The result must be the fullest development in a created aesthetic form of an original moment of insight, and it does not matter whether genius devotes a lifetime to producing a small result if that result be immortal. The difference between two types of genius is that one type (the Mozartian) is able to plunge the greatest depths of his own experience by the tremendous effort of a moment, the other (the Beethovenian) must dig deeper and deeper into his consciousness, layer by layer. What counts in either case is the vision which sees and pursues and attains the end; the logic of the artistic purpose.

A poet may be divinely gifted with a lucid and intense and purposive intellect; he may be clumsy and slow; that does not matter, what matters is integrity of purpose and the ability to maintain the purpose without losing oneself. Myself, I am scarcely capable of immediate concentration in poetry. My mind is not clear, my will is weak, I suffer from an excess of ideas and a weak sense of form. For every poem that I begin to write, I think of at least ten which I do not write down at all. For every poem which I do write down, there are seven or eight which I never complete.

The method which I adopt therefore is to write down as many ideas as possible, in however rough a form, in notebooks (I have at least twenty of these, on a shelf beside my desk, going back over fifteen years). I then make use of some of the sketches and discard others.

The best way of explaining how I develop the rough ideas which I use, is to take an example. Here is a notebook begun in 1944. About a hundred pages of it are covered with writing, and from this have emerged about six poems. Each idea, when it first occurs, is given a number. Sometimes the ideas do not get beyond one line. For example No. 3 (never developed) is the one line:

> *A language of flesh and roses*

I shall return to this line in a few pages, when I speak of inspiration. For the moment, I turn to No. 13, because here is an idea which has been developed to its conclusion. The first sketch begins thus:

> (a) *There are some days when the sea lies like a harp*
> *Stretched flat beneath the cliffs. The waves*
> *Like wires burn with the sun's copper glow*
> *(all the murmuring blue every silent)*
> *Between whose spaces every image*
> *Of sky* (field and) *hedge and field and boat*
> *Dwells like the huge face of the afternoon.*
> (Lies)
> *When the heat grows tired, the afternoon*
> *Out of the land may breathe a sigh*

(Across these wires like a hand. They vibrate
With)
Which moves across those wires like a soft hand
(Then the vibration)
Between whose spaces the vibration holds
Every bird-cry, dog's bark, man-shout
And creak of rollock from the land and sky
With all the music of the afternoon.

Obviously these lines are attempts to sketch out an idea which exists clearly enough on some level of the mind where it yet eludes the attempt to state it. At this stage, a poem is like a face which one seems to be able to visualize clearly in the eye of memory, but when one examines it mentally or tries to think it out, feature by feature, it seems to fade.

The idea of this poem is a vision of the sea. The faith of the poet is that if this vision is clearly stated, it will be significant. The vision is of the sea stretched under a cliff. On top of the cliff there are fields, hedges, houses. Horses draw carts along lanes, dogs bark far inland, bells ring in the distance. The shore seems laden with hedges, roses, horses, and men, all high above the sea, on a very fine summer day when the ocean seems to reflect and absorb the shore. Then the small strung-out glittering waves of the sea lying under the shore are like the strings of a harp which catch the sunlight. Between these strings lies the reflection of the shore. Butterflies are wafted out over the waves, which they mistake for the fields of the chalky landscape, searching them for flowers. On a day such as this, the land, reflected in the sea, appears to enter into the sea, as though it lies under it, like Atlantis. The wires of the harp are like a seen music fusing seascape and landscape.

Looking at this vision in another way, it obviously has symbolic value. The sea represents death and eternity, the land represents the brief life of the summer and of one human generation which passes into the sea of eternity. But let me here say at once that although the poet may be conscious of this aspect of his vision, it is exactly what he wants to avoid stating, or even being too concerned with. His job is to recreate his vision, and let it speak its moral for itself. The poet must distinguish clearly in his own mind between that which most definitely must be said and that which must not be said. The unsaid inner meaning is revealed in the music and the tonality of the poem, and the poet is conscious of it in his knowledge that a certain tone of voice, a certain rhythm, are necessary.

In the next twenty versions of the poem I felt my way towards the clarification of the seen picture, the music and the inner feeling. In the first version quoted above, there is the phrase in the second and third lines

The waves
Like wires burn with the sun's copper glow.

This phrase fuses the image of the sea with the idea of music, and it is therefore a key-phrase, because the theme of the poem is the fusion of the land with the sea. Here, then, are several versions of these one and a quarter lines, in the order in which they were written:

> (*b*) *The waves are wires*
> *Burning as with the secret song of fires*

> (*c*) *The day burns in the trembling wires*
> *With a vast music golden in the eyes*

> (*d*) *The day glows on its trembling wires*
> *Singing a golden music in the eyes*

> (*e*) *The day glows on its burning wires*
> *Like waves of music golden to the eyes.*

> (*f*) *Afternoon burns upon its wires*
> *Lines of music dazzling the eyes*

> (*g*) *Afternoon gilds its tingling wires*
> *To a visual silent music of the eyes*

In the final version, these two lines appear as in the following stanza:

> (*h*) *There are some days the happy ocean lies*
> *Like an unfingered harp, below the land.*
> *Afternoon gilds all the silent wires*
> *Into a burning music of the eyes.*
>
> *On mirroring paths between those fine-strung fires*
> *The shore, laden with roses, horses, spires,*
> *Wanders in water, imaged above ribbed sand.*

INSPIRATION

The hard work evinced in these examples, which are only a fraction of the work put into the whole poem, may cause the reader to wonder whether there is no such thing as inspiration, or whether it is merely Stephen Spender who is uninspired. The answer is that everything in poetry is work except inspiration, whether this work is achieved at one swift stroke, as Mozart wrote his music, or whether it is a slow process of evolution from stage to stage. Here again, I have to qualify the word 'work', as I qualified the word 'concentration': the work on a line of poetry may take the form of putting a version aside for a few days, weeks, or years, and then taking it up again, when it may be found that the line has, in the interval of time, almost rewritten itself.

Inspiration is the beginning of a poem and it is also its final goal. It is the first idea which drops into the poet's mind and it is the final idea which he at last achieves in words. In between this start and this winning post there is the hard race, the sweat and toil.

Paul Valéry speaks of the '*une ligne donnée*' of a poem. One line is given to the poet by God or by nature, the rest he has to discover for himself.

My own experience of inspiration is certainly that of a line or a phrase or a word or sometimes something still vague, a dim cloud of an idea which I feel must be condensed into a shower of words. The peculiarity of the key word or line is that it does not merely attract, as, say, the word 'braggadocio' attracts. It occurs in what seems to be an active, male, germinal form as though it were the centre of a statement requiring a beginning and an end, and as though it had an impulse in a certain direction. Here are examples:

> *A language of flesh and roses.*

This phrase (not very satisfactory in itself) brings to my mind a whole series of experiences and the idea of a poem which I shall perhaps write some years hence. I was standing in the corridor of a train passing through the Black Country. I saw a landscape of pits and pit-heads, artificial mountains, jagged yellow wounds in the earth, everything transformed as though by the toil of an enormous animal or giant tearing up the earth in search of prey or treasure. Oddly enough, a stranger next to me in the corridor echoed my inmost thought. He said: 'Everything there is manmade.' At this moment the line flashed into my head:

> *A language of flesh and roses*

The sequence of my thought was as follows: the industrial landscape which seems by now a routine and act of God which enslaves both employers and workers who serve and profit by it, is actually the expression of man's will. Men willed it to be so, and pit-heads, slag-heaps, and the ghastly disregard of anything but the pursuit of wealth, are a symbol of modern man's mind. In other words, the world which we create—the world of slums and telegrams and newspapers—is a kind of language of our inner wishes and thoughts. Although this is so, it is obviously a language which has got outside our control. It is a confused language, an irresponsible senile gibberish. This thought greatly distressed me, and I started thinking that if the phenomena created by humanity are really like words in a language, what kind of language do we really aspire to? All this sequence of thought flashed into my mind with the answer which came before the question: *A language of flesh and roses.*

I hope this example will give the reader some idea of what I mean by inspiration. Now the line, which I shall not repeat again, is a way of thinking imaginatively. If the line embodies some of the ideas which I have related above, these ideas must be further made clear in other lines. That is the terrifying challenge of poetry. Can I think out the logic of images? How easy it is to explain here the poem that I would have liked to write! How difficult it would be to write it. For writing it would imply living my way through the imaged experience of all these ideas, which here are mere abstractions, and such an effort of imaginative experience requires a lifetime of patience and watching.

Here is an example of a cloudy form of thought germinated by the word *cross*, which is the key word of the poem which exists formlessly in my mind. Recently my wife had a son. On the first day that I visited her after the boy's birth, I went by bus to the hospital. Passing through the streets on top of the bus, they all seemed very clean, and the thought occurred to me that everything was prepared for our child. Past generations have toiled so that any child born today inherits, with his generation, cities, streets, organization, the most elaborate machinery for living. Everything has been provided for him by people dead long before he was born. Then, naturally enough, sadder thoughts coloured this picture for me, and I reflected how he also inherited vast maladjustments, vast human wrongs. Then I thought of the child as like a pinpoint of present existence, the moment incarnate, in whom the whole of the past, and all possible futures *cross*. This word *cross* somehow suggested the whole situation to me of a child born into the world and also of the form of a poem about his situation. When the word *cross* appeared in the poem, the idea of the past should give place to the idea of the future and it should be apparent that the *cross* in which present and future meet is the secret of an individual human existence. And here again, the unspoken secret which lies beyond the poem, the moral significance of other meanings of the word *cross* begins to glow with its virtue that should never be said and yet should shine through every image in the poem.

This account of inspiration is probably weak beside the accounts that other poets might give. I am writing of my own experience, and my own inspiration seems to me like the faintest flash of insight into the nature of reality beside that of other poets whom I can think of. However, it is possible that I describe here a kind of experience which, however slight it may be, is perhaps truer to the real poetic experience than Aldous Huxley's account of how a young poet writes poetry in his novel *Time Must Have a Stop*.

MEMORY

If the art of concentrating in a particular way is the discipline necessary for poetry to reveal itself, memory exercised in a particular way is the natural gift of poetic genius. The poet, above all else, is a person who never forgets certain sense-impressions which he has experienced and which he can re-live again and again as though with all their original freshness.

All poets have this highly developed sensitive apparatus of memory, and they are usually aware of experiences which happened to them at the earliest age and which retain their pristine significance throughout life. The meeting of Dante and Beatrice when the poet was only nine years of age is the experience which became a symbol in Dante's mind around which the *Divine Comedy* crystallized. The experience of nature which forms the subject of Wordsworth's poetry was an extension of a childhood vision of 'natural presences' which surrounded the boy Wordsworth. And his decision in later life to live in the Lake District was a decision to return to the scene of these childhood memories which were the most important experiences in his poetry. There is evidence for the importance of this kind of memory in all the creative arts, and the argument certainly applies to prose which is creative. Sir Osbert Sitwell has told me that his book *Before the Bombardment,* which contains an extremely civilized and satiric account of the social life of Scarborough before and during the 1914–18 war, was based on his observations of life in that resort before he had reached the age of twelve.

It therefore is not surprising that although I have no memory for telephone numbers, addresses, faces, and where I have put this morning's correspondence, I have a perfect memory for the sensation of certain experiences which are crystallized for me around certain associations. I could demonstrate this from my own life by the overwhelming nature of associations which, suddenly aroused, have carried me back so completely into the past, particularly into my childhood, that I have lost all sense of the present time and place. But the best proofs of this power of memory are found in the odd lines of poems written in notebooks fifteen years ago. A few fragments of unfinished poems enable me to enter immediately into the experiences from which they were derived, the circumstances in which they were written, and the unwritten feelings in the poem that were projected but never put into words.

> *. . . Knowledge of a full sun*
> *That runs up his big sky, above*
> *The hill, then in those trees and throws*
> *His smiling on the turf.*

That is an incomplete idea of fifteen years ago, and I remember exactly a balcony of a house facing a road, and, on the other side of the road, pine trees, beyond which lay the sea. Every morning the sun sprang up, first of all above the horizon of the sea, then it climbed to the tops of the trees and shone on my window. And this memory connects with the sun that shines through my window in London now in spring and early summer. So that the memory is not exactly a memory. It is more like one prong upon which a whole calendar of similar experiences happening throughout years, collect. A memory once clearly stated ceases to be a memory, it becomes perpetually present, because every time we experience something which recalls it, the clear and lucid original experience imposes its formal beauty on the new experiences. It is thus no longer a memory but an experience lived through again and again.

As I turn over these old notebooks, my eye catches some lines, in a projected long poem, which immediately reshape themselves into the following short portrait of a woman's face:

> Her eyes are gleaming fish
> Caught in her nervous face, as if in a net.
> Her hair is wild and fair, haloing her cheeks
> Like a fantastic flare of Southern sun.
> There is madness in her cherishing her children.
> Sometimes, perhaps a single time in years,
> Her wandering fingers stoop to arrange some flowers—
> Then in her hands her whole life stops and weeps.

It is perhaps true to say that memory is the faculty of poetry, because the imagination itself is an exercise of memory. There is nothing we imagine which we do not already know. And our ability to imagine is our ability to remember what we have already once experienced and to apply it to some different situation. Thus the greatest poets are those with memories so great that they extend beyond their strongest experiences to their minutest observations of people and things far outside their own self-centredness (the weakness of memory is its self-centredness: hence the narcisistic nature of most poetry).

Here I can detect my own worst weakness. My memory is defective and self-centred. I lack the confidence in using it to create situations outside myself, although I believe that, in theory, there are very few situations in life which a poet should not be able to imagine, because it is a fact that most poets have experienced almost every situation in life. I do not mean by this that a poet who writes about a Polar expedition has actually been to the North Pole. I mean, though, that he has been cold, hungry, etc., so that it is possible for him by remembering imaginatively his own felt experiences to know what it is like to explore the North Pole. That is where I fail. I cannot write about going to the North Pole.

FAITH

It is evident that a faith in their vocation, mystical in intensity, sustains poets. There are many illustrations from the lives of poets to show this, and Shakespeare's sonnets are full of expressions of his faith in the immortality of his lines.

From my experience I can clarify the nature of this faith. When I was nine, we went to the Lake District, and there my parents read me some of the poems of Wordsworth. My sense of the sacredness of the task of poetry began then, and I have always felt that a poet's was a sacred vocation, like a saint's. Since I was nine, I have wanted to be various things, for example, Prime Minister (when I was twelve). Like some other poets I am attracted by the life of power and the life of action, but I am still more repelled by them. Power involves forcing oneself upon the attention of historians by doing things and occupying offices which are, in themselves, important, so that what is truly powerful is not the soul of a so-called powerful and prominent man but the position which he fills and the things which he does. Similarly, the life of 'action' which seems so very positive is, in fact, a selective, even a negative kind of life. A man of action does one thing or several things because he does not do something else. Usually men who do very spectacular things fail completely to do the ordinary things which fill the lives of most normal people, and which would be far more heroic and spectacular perhaps, if they did not happen to be done by many people. Thus in practice the life of action has always seemed to me an act of cutting oneself off from life.

Although it is true that poets are vain and ambitious, their vanity and ambition are of the purest kind attainable in this world, for the saint re-nounces ambition. They are ambitious to be accepted for what they ultimately are as revealed by their inmost experiences, their finest perceptions, their deepest feelings, their uttermost sense of truth, in their poetry. They cannot cheat about these things, because the quality of their own being is revealed not in the noble sentiments which their poetry expresses, but in sensibility, control of language, rhythm and music, things which cannot be attained by a vote of confidence from an electorate, or by the office of Poet Laureate. Of course, work is tremendously important, but, in poetry, even the greatest labour can only serve to reveal the intrinsic qualities of soul of the poet as he really is.

Since there can be no cheating, the poet, like the saint, stands in all his works before the bar of a perpetual day of judgment. His vanity of course is pleased by success, though even success may contribute to his understanding that popularity does not confer on him the favourable judgment of all the ages which he seeks. For what does it mean to be praised by one's own age, which is soaked in crimes and stupidity, except perhaps that future ages, wise where we are foolish, will see him as a typical expression of this age's crimes and stupidity? Nor is lack of success a guarantee of great poetry, though there are some who pretend that it is. Nor can the critics, at any rate beyond a certain limited point of technical judgment, be trusted.

The poet's faith is therefore, firstly, a mystique of vocation, secondly, a faith in his own truth, combined with his own devotion to a task. There can really be no greater faith than the confidence that one is doing one's utmost to fulfil one's high vocation, and it is this that has inspired all the greatest poets. At the same time this faith is coupled with a deep humility because one knows that, ultimately, judgment does not rest with oneself. All one can do is to achieve nakedness, to be what one is with all one's faculties and perceptions, strengthened by all the skill which one can acquire, and then to stand before the judgment of time.

In my notebooks, I find the following Prose Poem, which expresses these thoughts:

> *Bring me peace bring me power bring me assurance. Let me reach the bright day, the high chair, the plain desk, where my hand at last controls the words, where anxiety no longer undermines me. If I don't reach these I'm thrown to the wolves, I'm a restless animal wandering from place to place, from experience to experience.*
>
> *Give me the humility and the judgment to live alone with the deep and rich satisfaction of my own creating: not to be thrown into doubt by a word of spite or disapproval.*
>
> *In the last analysis don't mind whether your work is good or bad so long as it has the completeness, the enormity of the whole world which you love.*

SONG

Inspiration and song are the irreducible final qualities of a poet which make his vocation different from all others. Inspiration is an experience in which a line or an idea is given to one, and perhaps also a state of mind in which one writes one's best poetry. Song is far more difficult to define. It is the music which a poem as yet unthought of will assume, the empty womb of poetry forever in the poet's consciousness, waiting for the fertilizing seed.

Sometimes, when I lie in a state of half-waking half-sleeping, I am conscious of a stream of words which seem to pass through my mind, without their having a meaning, but they have a sound, a sound of passion, or a sound recalling poetry that I know. Again sometimes when I am writing, the music of the words I am trying to shape takes me far beyond the words, I am aware of a rhythm, a dance, a fury, which is as yet empty of words.

In these observations, I have said little about headaches, midnight oil, pints of beer or of claret, love affairs, and so on, which are supposed to be stations on the journeys of poets through life. There is no doubt that writing poetry, when a poem appears to succeed, results in an intense physical excitement, a sense of release and ecstasy. On the other hand, I dread writing poetry, for, I suppose, the following reasons: a poem is a terrible journey, a painful effort of concentrating the imagination; words are an extremely difficult medium to use, and sometimes when one has spent days trying to say a thing clearly one finds that one has only said it dully; above all, the writing of a poem brings one face to face with one's own personality with all its familiar and clumsy limitations. In every other phase of existence, one can exercise the orthodoxy of a conventional routine: one can be polite to one's friends, one can get through the day at the office, one can pose, one can draw attention to one's position in society, one is—in a word—dealing with men. In poetry, one is wrestling with a god.

Usually, when I have completed a poem, I think 'this is my best poem', and I wish to publish it at once. This is partly because I only write when I have something new to say, which seems more worth while than what I have said before, partly because optimism about my present and future makes me despise my past. A few days after I have finished a poem, I relegate it to the past of all my other wasted efforts, all the books I do not wish to open.

Perhaps the greatest pleasure I have got from poems that I have written is when I have heard some lines quoted which I have not at once recognized. And I have thought 'how good and how interesting', before I have realized that they are my own.

In common with other creative writers I pretend that I am not, and I am, exceedingly affected by unsympathetic criticism, whilst praise usually makes me suspect that the reviewer does not know what he is talking about. Why are writers so sensitive to criticism? Partly, because it is their business to be sensitive, and they are sensitive about this as about other things. Partly, because every serious creative writer is really in his heart concerned with reputation and not with success (the most successful writer I have known, Sir Hugh Walpole, was far and away the most unhappy about his reputation, because the 'highbrows' did not like him). Again, I suspect that every writer is secretly writing for *someone*, probably for a parent or teacher who did not believe in him in childhood. The critic who refuses to 'understand' immediately becomes identified with this person, and the understanding of many admirers only adds to the writer's secret bitterness if this one refusal persists.

Gradually one realizes that there is always this someone who will not like one's work. Then, perhaps, literature becomes a humble exercise of faith in being all that one can be in one's art, of being more than oneself, expecting little, but with a faith in the mystery of poetry which gradually expands into a faith in the mysterious service of truth.

Yet what failures there are! And how much mud sticks to one; mud not thrown by other people but acquired in the course of earning one's living, answering or not answering the letters which one receives, supporting or not supporting public causes. All one can hope is that this mud is composed of little grains of sand which will produce pearls.

William Carlos Williams   has become one of America's most influential poets. Using a career in medicine to support his literary interests, he wrote novels, short stories, essays, plays, and an autobiography over a period of fifty years, beginning with his privately printed *Poems* in 1909, and including his most critically admired works, the epic poem, *Patterson* (four volumes: 1946–1958) and *Pictures from Brueghel and Other Poems* (1962). Among many honors, he was appointed to the Chair of Poetry at the Library of Congress. Originally influenced by French imagist painters, he eventually called for a revolution in poetry in which there would be "no ideas but in things." After his death in 1963, he was posthumously awarded the Pulitzer Prize and the Gold Medal for Poetry by the National Institute of Arts and Letters.

How To Write

William Carlos Williams

One takes a piece of paper, anything, the flat of a shingle, slate, cardboard and with anything handy to the purpose begins to put down the words after the desired expression in mind. This is the anarchical phase of writing. The blankness of the writing surface may cause the mind to shy, it may be impossible to release the faculties. Write, write anything: it is all in all probability worthless anyhow, it is never hard to destroy written characters. But it is absolutely essential to the writing of anything worth while that the mind be fluid and release itself to the task.

Forget all rules, forget all restrictions, as to taste, as to what ought to be said, write for the pleasure of it—whether slowly or fast—every form of resistance to a complete release should be abandoned.

For today we know the meaning of depth; it is a primitive profundity of the personality that must be touched if what we do is to have it. The faculties, untied, proceed backward through the night of our unconscious past. It goes down to the ritualistic, amoral past of the race, to fetish, to dream to wherever the "genius" of the particular writer finds itself able to go.

At such a time the artist (the writer) may well be thought of as a dangerous person. Anything may turn up. He has no connection with ordered

Source: *William Carlos Williams*, Interviews with William Carlos Williams: "Speaking Straight Ahead." *Copyright by the Estate of William Carlos Williams. Reprinted by permission of New Directions.*

society. He may perform an imbecility or he may by a freak of mind penetrate with tremendous value to society into some avenue long closed or never yet opened. But he is disconnected with any orderly advance or purpose.

It is now that artists stoutly defend themselves against any usefulness in their art. And it makes no difference whether it is a treatise on mathematics or a poem that is being written. *While* it is being written, as far as possible, the writer be he mathematician or poet, must with a stored mind no doubt, must nevertheless thoroughly abandon himself to the writing in greater or less degree if he wishes to clinch his expression with any depth of significance.

The demonic power of the mind is its racial and individual past, it is the rhythmic ebb and flow of the mysterious life process and unless this is tapped by the writer nothing of moment can result. It is the reason for the value of poetry whose unacknowledged rhythmic symbolism is its greatest strength and which makes all prose in comparison with it little more than the patter of the intelligence.

So poets have been considered unbalanced creatures (as they often are), madmen very often. But the intrinsic reason for this is seldom understood. They are in touch with "voices," but this is the very essence of their power, the voices are the past, the depths of our very beings. It is the deeper, not "lower" (in the usually silly sense) portions of the personality speaking, the middle brain, the nerves, the glands, the very muscles and bones of the body itself speaking.

But once the writing is on the paper it becomes an object. It is no longer a fluid speaking through a symbolism of ritualistic forms but definite words on a piece of paper. It has now left the region of the formative past and come up to the present. It has entered now a new field, that of intelligence. I do not say that the two fields do not somewhat overlap at times but the chief characteristic of the writing now is that it is an object for the liveliest attention that the full mind can give it and that there has been a change in the whole situation.

It is this part of writing that is dealt with in the colleges and in all forms of teaching but nowhere does it seem to be realized that without its spring from the deeper strata of the personality all the teaching and learning in the world can make nothing of the result. Not to have realized this is the greatest fault of those who think they know something of the art.

All that the first phase of writing has accomplished is to place its record on the paper. Is this valuable, is it worthless? These questions it cannot answer and it is of no use for the poet to say: This is what I have done, therefore it is excellent. He may say that and what he has done may be excellent but the reasons should be made clear and they involve the conscious intelligence.

The written object comes under the laws of all created things involving a choice and once the choice has been made there must be an exercise of the will to back it. One goes forward carefully. But the first step must not be to make what has been written under a quasi-hallucinatory state conform to rules. What rules? Rather the writing should be carefully examined for the new and the extraordinary and nothing rejected without clear reason. For in this way the intelligence itself is corrected.

Thus, we know that in language is anchored most of all of the wisdom and follies of our lives. Besides which language may grow stale, meanings may and will be lost, phrases may block our arrival at conclusion. And in the writings of genius, in the poems (if any) the released personality of the artist the very break with stupidity which we are seeking may have occurred. And this will always be in the *form* which the first writing has taken.

But lest a mistake occur I am not speaking of two persons, a poet and a critic, I am speaking of the same person, the writer. He has written with his deepest mind, now the object is there and he is attacking it with his most recent mind, the fore-brain, the seat of memory and ratiocination, the so-called intelligence.

This cannot do more in reviewing that which is before it than reject that which has been said better elsewhere. Whereas in the first phase a man need not seriously have written at all, now it is necessary that he know the work of other men, in other times, as much as possible and from every available angle. This is the student's moment.

And for an American there is one great decision to be made. What language is being written?

A few years ago some American in England wrote an attack upon American writers living in America saying in effect; How can they write English not hearing it spoken every day?—His comment was meant to be ironical but it turned out to be naive. The answer to his question is, naturally: Why bother with English when we have a language of our own?

It is the intelligence which gives us the history of writing and its point of arrival today, the place of Poe, the value of Whitman, the purpose of free verse, why it occurred at just that time, the significance of Gertrude Stein's work, that of the writings of James Joyce and the rationale of modern verse structure.

Briefly all this is the birth of a new language. It is a new allotment of significance. It is the cracking up of phrases which have stopped the mind.

All these things could be gone into in detail, a book could be written and must be written of them, but that is not my purpose here. What I have undertaken is to show the two great phases of writing without either of which the work accomplished can hardly be called mastery. And that, in the phrase of James Joyce, is the he and the she of it.

Concentration

. . . in order to illuminate for others, one must obviously first be able to see for himself. Seeing is my key word, seeing with the heart, with the brain, with the eye. . . . Normally we see others only as they relate to our own immediate needs, and for that, normal vision is often sufficient. Yet there are times when we have a need we cannot recognize, a sudden hunger to know what lies in the heart of others.

Edward Lewis Wallant

Paul Engle, poet, novelist, and editor, received his M.A. from the State University of Iowa. His thesis, a collection of poems, is thought to be the first work of imaginative writing in America to be awarded an advanced degree. It was later published as *Worn Earth* (1932) by the Yale Series of Younger Poets. Engle returned to Iowa where he founded and directed the Iowa Writers' Program in creative writing; he is credited with promoting the work of younger poets throughout the United States. *American Child: Sonnets for my Daughter* (1956) and *American Song* (1979) are among his most admired works.

Salt Crystals, Spider Webs, and Words

Paul Engle

Writing is like making love—it is astonishing how far pure instinct (if it really is pure) will carry you. It is also true of both these lyrical forms of expression that a few things consciously learned will push toward perfection what might otherwise be an ordinary act.

And yet—can writing actually be taught? Is there much more you can give to a beginner beyond Flaubert's no-nonsense advice of a kiss on the brow and a kick in the behind?

In pointing out that a writer crystallizes a concept, as when he endows a woman with qualities she simply does not have, Stendhal produced an image that, however little it flatters the ladies, does dramatize the process by which persuasive words can turn a dull object into something glittering and gay. He observes that a dead branch, dark and ugly, if left overnight in the salt mines of Salzburg, will be covered with crystals and next day will glitter in the sunlight.

This image of the salt crystals on the branch wisely and attractively illustrates what the writer does with that curious and secret substance called his "material." What writer has not been stopped by an eager-eyed and bushy-

Source: *From* On Creative Writing *by Paul Engle. Copyright © 1963, 1964 by Paul Engle. Reprinted by permission of the Publisher, E. P. Dutton.*

tailed person who cries out despairingly, "I've got the greatest material for a book, if I could just *write!*"

The first and most important point about writing is that there is no such thing as material by itself, apart from the way in which a person sees it, feels toward it, and is able to give it organized form and expression in words. For a writer, form is a part of content, affecting it, realizing it. A man may go through the most dramatic and horrible experiences in war, but actually draw out of them less "material" for writing than shy Emily Dickinson in the second-floor room of an Amherst house, lowering notes in baskets out the window and thinking gently of death—or even (biographers speculate) of a man she knew but little, whom she might never see again.

Henry James said it first and beautifully when he wrote that experience is unlimited: "an immense sensibility, a kind of huge spider web of the finest silken threads suspended in the chamber of consciousness, and catching every air-borne particle in its tissue. It is the very atmosphere of the mind." This is crucial, for it is not what happens in the outside world that is of absolute significance, but what happens to that external event when it is discovered and then ordered by the internal power of a mind. James goes on to speak then of the creative aspect: "and when the mind is imaginative . . . it takes to itself the faintest hints of life, it converts the very pulse of the air into revelations."

By experience, then, a writer does not mean having adventures. In answering a critic who had complained about the novel that it is impossible to have one without bold action, James protested, "Why without adventure, more than without matrimony, or celibacy, or parturition, or cholera . . . ?"

Anything is suitable for fiction, which is not a record of incidents happening *to* men and women, but of the response they make within themselves to the incidents. This is because fiction deals with character, which determines action, and thus actions illustrate character. The conduct of a man in a ring fighting an enraged bull or the soft wave of a woman's hand are equally moving and suitable.

A thousand Frenchmen may walk down a Paris street and, turning a corner, forget the place. But Toulouse-Lautrec walking down the same street would see, with his shrewd eye, and remember, with his artist's force of retention, not bricks but visions. In this way the imagination works not only on the stuff that is stored in the mind, but also on the very act of experiencing. Like the pilot, the writer must see faster and more completely than the ordinary viewer of life.

Out of his practical skills in the writing of fiction, James described the process of the writer using his experience. "The power to guess the unseen from the seen," he said, "to trace the implication of things, to judge the whole piece by the pattern, the condition of feeling life in general so completely that you are well on your way to knowing any particular corner of it—this cluster of gifts may almost be said to constitute experience, and they occur in country and in town, and in the most differing stages of education. If experience consists of impressions, it may be said that impressions *are* experience, just as (have we not seen it?) they are the very air we breathe."

This is final wisdom about writing. The writer, when given an inch, takes an ell. Remember that an ell is forty-five inches. If that is the degree of heightening, then the eye of the writer must look at life with forty-five times as much perception. That is a marvelous degree of intensity, and in particular when it comes from the author of *Portrait of a Lady*, a book about which it has been remarked that, although it concerns the relationship between a man and a woman, there is only one kiss, and the heroine, poor thing, did not enjoy it.

But some will argue: writing, like all art, is intuitive, and any intrusion of the reason will destroy the lovely, natural thing. This is dead wrong. It reduces writing to the level of a child babbling without regard to the shape of what he is saying. It is, indeed, so much like the uninhibited confessions from the psychiatrist's couch, sodium amytal cheerfully flowing through the veins and breaking down shyness, that it would seem proper to give inhibition-removing drugs to the writer. He could sit there gaily listening to the rustlings of his unconscious. And of course the hallucinatory state would be the most creative of all.

It is quite possible that some good things could be thus spontaneously created. I met in India people who could induce visions. Yet surely the great and structured works of writing are done with the intelligence playing over against the intuition, each bracing the other, the mind giving form and sense, the intuition giving immediacy of impression, the stored-up memory, the deeply instinctive phrase.

To say that writing comes only from the intuition is to belittle it as coming from one narrow aspect of our lives alone. The opposite is true. The total life of the writer is the source of his work. All these go into his writing, in varying quantities: the senses, as of taste and touch, the rate of metabolism, the blood pressure, the digestion, the body temperature, the memory of things past, perhaps going back to the childhood not only of the writer but of the race itself, the liveliness and alertness of the brain, previous reading of books, shrewdness of insight into human character, the libido, the ear for the sound of language.

The writer, therefore, must not only have a more than ordinary capacity for life and the power to retain what he experiences in a readily available memory but he must also have an astonishing degree of self-knowledge. Unless he is aware of his material, he cannot use it, save for the always present quantity that flows up from the deep well of the unconscious recollection. Without access to knowledge of self, the writer can make dreams but not art. Dr. Lawrence S. Kubie says that without self-knowledge, "we can have the neurotic raw material of literature, but not mature literature. We can have no adults, but only aging children who are armed with words."

By self-knowledge I do not mean self-expression. Although all good writing always bears the individual mark, sound, and motion of the writer, he is not trying to put his own self into words, but to create a piece of writing.

Often, the less of his own self involved or expressed, the better. His own personality ought to be dissolved into the images or characters of his book. The writer is offering us not reality, but his reaction to whatever reality he has experienced.

Yet the ego is important. It must be that within the creative person there is a constant tension between an awareness of the reality around him, a thrusting up of the unconscious life and its memory, and the drive of the ego toward controlling these in a form that also heightens them. These are crude terms to describe subtle conditions, but the creation of any art is one of the most complex of human activities, involving every animal and human quality. The ego must shape the mortal impulses. It is here that something can indeed be taught about writing, for it is in this shaping that the individual's private events are turned into public forms. It is here that writing becomes an art and not merely a report on experience, and this is true of the best reporting.

How many boys have played around greenhouses? Swarms. But how many, on growing up, have put their feelings about that place into powerful poetry? Only Theodore Roethke. His account is proof.

Roethke asks what does it matter that he grew up in and around a beautiful greenhouse, hated school, worked in a pickle factory, lived sometimes quietly and sometimes foolishly and violently, and meant almost nothing to the people of his own state, the man in the street, but passionately desired their regard?

> All such details, and others like them [Roethke comments] seem particularly trivial and vulgar in my case because I have tried to put down in poems, as barely and honestly as possible, symbolically, what few nuggets of observation and, let us hope, spiritual wisdom I have managed to seize upon in the course of a conventional albeit sometimes disordered existence. I have tried to transmute and purify my "life," the sense of being defiled by it in both small and formal and somewhat blunt short poems, and latterly, in longer poems which try in their rhythms to catch the very movement of the mind itself, to trace the spiritual history of a protagonist (not "I" personally) of all haunted and harried men; to make in this series (now probably finished) a true and not arbitrary order which will permit many ranges of feeling, including humor. . . .

And then he says in verse:

> My heart sways with the world.
> I am that final thing,
> A man learning to sing.

Although this may suggest a self-consciousness not shared by all poets, it is further evidence of that deep need for self-knowledge that is a strength and a source. Roethke knew *what* he was trying to do in those moving and often tortured poems, and this awareness, far from inhibiting the imaginative free-dom of the verse, enriched it. The cool mind, curiously enough, it seems, really can express a warm feeling.

Once the writer has a sense of his experience and of his own self, without illusion, and can be tough-minded about his own weakness and vulgarity, what else can he possibly learn? What can he *do* to make his writing better, assuming that he is not trapped in the conviction that writing is a wholly automatic outburst from underground?

He can examine the knowledge of their own writing habits great men have made available. It is odd the things writers have done. The German poet Schiller used to keep rotting apples under the lid of his desk because their smell helped him write. Pilots on the river at Rouen would see the light in Flaubert's study very late at night as he utterly shut himself away from the world to worry two pages of prose a week into the ruthlessly purified and perfected shape he demanded. Why this enormous care? The old wisecrack says that a physician who fails can always bury his patient out of sight. Frank Lloyd Wright remarked that an architect who fails can at least urge his client to plant vines. The writer, however, once his work is in print, can do nothing. There the text is, black on the page; any errors and ugliness will show forever. There are rare exceptions, of course, like William Butler Yeats, who, in his old age (with that marvelous lyrical mind hardened by the criticism of others), went back to the poems of his youth and cut out much of the sentimentality and soft, vague language.

Reticient as always, William Faulkner said that the tools of the writer's trade are paper, tobacco, food, and whiskey. Of these, the most dangerous is not tobacco or whiskey (writers are famous for abusing them), but paper. One of the most terrifying sights is that waiting, threatening blank sheet. Its force is proved by the Japanese writer who, after much success, could not, for a long time, push ahead with his writing. One autumn—and this is a true story—he disappeared. The next spring his body was found, after the snow had melted, high up in the mountains. Pinned to his jacket was a note only the suffering writer could have written: "I have done this because I could no longer endure the sight of the empty page."

All those writers who have commented on their craft agree that a work of art is work. How could the joining of passion and idea in slippery words be anything but a labor? That first really modern novel, *Madame Bovary*, was composed by Gustave Flaubert with the deliberation of a medieval monk illuminating a manuscript. The French novelist could write quickly and fluently, as his early books and his lively letters show, but he would never give up a sentence until it was beyond improving. To get his description of the landscape correct, he sat all day on a balcony looking through pieces of different-colored glass in order to note the changes in shape of fields and roads and trees hour by hour.

Never was a writer more emotionally involved with what he was writing than Flaubert. When he described Emma Bovary poisoning herself, he was so moved that he could taste arsenic on his own tongue and felt so poisoned himself that he vomited his dinner. And yet when he finally finished that scene, he had engineered it onto the page with an almost fanatical control. Once again, the writer's talent had produced an immortal passage out of passionate deliberation.

Flaubert would begin a single paragraph by setting down its general idea, with perhaps a few images (a risk always, for a brilliant image-making faculty he had; he wrote that he was devoured by metaphors as by vermin and spent his time crushing them). Then he wrote a first draft, reading it aloud for sound and sense (always read any sort of text out loud, the surest way to catch the feeble phrase, the trite adjective, the outworn image, the dull rhythm, the phony speech). Then he would rewrite, again and again, as a fine craftsman polishes over and over the same increasingly brilliant piece of maple or mahogany. Every word that did not act with energy was thrown away, until the paragraph was lean, tough, expressive. *Madame Bovary's* final version was written on 1,788 pages, but these were only the latest of many times that number of pages actually written. At times fifteen or twenty pages would be reduced to four. Thus, when Flaubert said that he spent a week over two pages, he meant over the two finally perfected pages out of many more.

Flaubert may be the only man in history who told his girl friend, "You should write more coldly." This was a part of his advice that "we must be on our guard against that kind of intellectual overheating called inspiration, which often consists more largely of nervous emotion than of muscular strength . . . my brow is burning, sentences keep rushing into my head. . . . Instead of one idea I have six, and where the most simple type of exposition is called for I find myself writing similes and metaphors. I could keep going until tomorrow noon without fatigue." And yet he could follow such an outburst with the blunt advise, brief, wise, but taking most writers a lifetime to learn: "Everything should be done coldly, with poise." When putting down the word "hysterics" one day he was so carried away that he bellowed loudly and felt so sharply what Emma Bovary was going through that he was afraid of having hysterics himself.

Can it be that the French, more than any other people, are able to balance heat and cold, desire and deliberation, and make a single intense but controlled utterance? The modern poet, Paul Valéry, wrote that poetry must be a holiday of the mind and then said, with greater calm, that when he writes, "I proceed like a surgeon who sterilizes his hands and prepares the area to be operated on . . . clearing up the verbal situation."

The English seem more practical, if a little less dedicated to perfection. Novelist Joyce Cary described his process thus:

A finished book of mine starts usually perhaps ten years before as a character sketch and a bit of description; it goes on to an incident or so, it gathers subsidiary characters, and then perhaps I grow interested in it, and set out to give it

form as a book. I sketch a plan; I may write the end, the middle, and the
beginning and very often just in this order. That is, I decide how and where the
book shall end, which is just as important to a book as to a play, and then I ask
myself where are the most difficult turns in the book. Then I may write one of
these difficult passages to see if it is viable. . . . I may stop there. But if it does
work, then I may devise a beginning and finish the book.

How contrary to the old notion of inspiration to find Cary devising a beginning of a novel of which he has written bits in various parts and without order. This is evidence that what the writer is really doing is not so much writing a poem or play or story that he has firmly in mind, but rather is using his writing to discover what it truly is he is trying to say. Often he will not know until the final revision of the last page what he had been trying to do from the start.

One would hardly guess the zest and liveliness of Chekhov's mind if he had only seen a moody performance of *The Sea Gull.* Commenting on the new "decadent" writers he noted, "They're a lot of strong, healthy young men: what they need is to be sentenced to a few months hard labor! This new-art business is just a pack of nonsense. . . . There's nothing new in art except talent." Chekhov constantly wrote subjects for stories in moments taken from his medical practice ("Medicine is my lawful wife, literature my mistress. When I am tired of the one, I spend a night with the other"). One notebook contained 100 entries. Some of these are diverting: A building contractor of great frugality loathed paying repair bills, When he married, he chose an exceptionally healthy woman so that he would have no repair bills with her.

A writer should be as objective as a chemist, he commented, and have nothing to do with the subjective approach that most of us make in our everyday lives. And when he wrote that the writer should never sit down to his work until he felt cold as ice, he was remarkably like Flaubert. Any reader of Chekhov's short stories will be amazed to find how very simple were the original notes for two of the finest. "A cabdriver who has just lost his son has to go on working just the same. He tries to speak of his grief to his fares, but finds only indifference." Another equally famous story began with three little sentences. "Some officers on maneuvers are invited to a house where there are several young women. One of them kisses one of the officers, a shy and reserved young man, in the dark. He looks for her, but in vain." These are the plain, experienced reality, but the stories written out of them are the heightened overreality.

Poor Chekhov, tending the sick with his own fatal illness corrupting his lungs. When he died in Germany, his coffin was taken to Muscow in a baggage car marked "Oysters." Yet he never allowed a scrap of self-pity to interfere with the absolute integrity of his dedication to writing:

My own experience is that once a story has been written, one has to cross out
the beginning and the end. It is there that we authors do most of our lying. . . .

One must always tear up the first half. I mean that seriously. Young writers begin by, as one says, "placing the story"—whereas the reader ought, on the contrary, to be able to grasp what it is all about by the way it is told, without any explanations from the author, from the conversation and the actions of the characters. . . . One must ruthlessly suppress everything that is not concerned with the subject. If, in the first chapter, you say there is a gun hanging on the wall, you should make quite sure that it is going to be used further on in the story.

Chekhov felt strongly the distinction between direct reality as it is lived and the imagined reality of art. In 1898 he went to a rehearsal of *The Sea Gull* at the Moscow Art Theater and was told by an actor that backstage there would be sounds of frogs croaking, grasshoppers scraping, and dogs barking. He asked why, and was told this would be realistic. But the theatre is not realism, it is art, he argued. If you put a real nose into a painting of a face, the nose will be realistic but the picture will be ruined. You do not use fiction to resolve the existence of God; you exhibit characters conducting lives and show the way in which they discuss God.

Similarly Tolstoy remarked that *Anna Karenina*, that massive novel, was just a simple story about a married woman who falls in love with an officer. This sort of reducing of any piece of writing to its essence is a part of that control over material which is indispensable to the practicing writer. Such definition comes out of enormous and confusing reaches of experience. No one has more imaginatively stated the mysterious and at the same time gritty nature of human existence than Virginia Woolf when she wrote that "life is a luminous halo, a semitransparent envelope surrounding us from the beginning."

Virginia Woolf also wrote a paragraph defining the nature of this envelope more precisely:

Examine for a moment an ordinary mind on an ordinary day. The mind receives myriad impressions—trivial, fantastic, evanescent, or engraved with the sharpness of steel. From all sides they come, an incessant shower of innumerable atoms; and as they fall, as they shape themselves into the life of Monday or Tuesday, the accent falls differently from of old; the moment of importance came not here but there; so that, if the writer were a freeman and not a slave, if he could write what he chose, not what he must, if he could base his work upon his own feeling and not upon convention, there would be no plot, no comedy, no tragedy, no love interest, or catastrophe in the accepted style.

The simple, often gruntlike puffs of air which we call words must be used by the writer with such skill that they can bring to a reader, who cannot even hear whatever tone of voice the writer would give them, a form and sense that will move him. This is by no means so easy as lifting bricks all day or breaking stone. Flaubert testifies to that: "My head reels and my throat aches with chasing after, slogging over, delving into, turning 'round, groping after, and bellowing, in a hundred thousand different ways, a sentence that I've at last finished. It's good . . . " One sentence!

No one knew better the tortures or the necessity of this sort of harsh self-discipline than that most exuberant and debauched poet, Baudelaire. In his *Flowers of Evil*, he wrote, there was a cold and sinister beauty. How did that beauty happen? This first of the beatniks differed from his later brothers not in his contempt for the vulgarity of middle-class life, nor in his concern for the flaunting immorality that repudiated such life, but in his attitude toward his art. Yearning to have his book appear so that it could prove to his mother, his formidable father-in-law General Aupick, and his friends that he was an authentic poet, he nevertheless kept the printer waiting several months while he revised a few lines into perfection. It may actually be that much writing is created into excellence and then revised into greatness. This is true of the play, the story, the novel, the poem, the article, of whatever form men choose to make words move other men.

Paul Horgan's work has been long associated with quality fiction and painstaking scholarship. A prolific writer and illustrator, he has published novels, poetry, history, essays, and children's books. In 1954 he was awarded both the Pulitzer Prize and Bancroft Prize for *Great River: The Rio Grande in North American History.* "The supreme act of self-respect in any society," he has written, "is to know its own origins, gather all possible evidence from them, and share them with an interested public in a form as appropriate and beautiful as possible." His most recent novel, *The Thin Mountain Air* (1977), takes its setting from Horgan's childhood experience in the southwest, as do most of his thirty-two other works.

Discipline and Vision

Paul Horgan

Any writer who undertakes to make his living by writing—and most writers hope to do so—must depend first of all on discipline in the simplest details as well as in the most exalted intentions of his task. This discipline he must earn for himself, for it is he, himself, and no one else, who will have to maintain it throughout all his professional life.

The first act of the writer's discipline is to serve an apprenticeship with humility and willingness to learn. I have taught certain aspects of my craft in various universities and I have never ceased being amazed at the almost unanimous expectation of students (graduate and undergraduate alike) who look to the publication and the success of the very first works they commit to paper. You cannot help being touched at their confidence, for you observe it through the eyes of memory. It is the blithe energy of youth working in their imaginations, rehearsing fame, wealth, and position; and you wish you could let their hopes be fulfilled, you wish this until—again through a backward glance—you recall that acceptance of devoted labor at the humblest details of learning how to write, no matter how long it may have to take, will be the best thing you could wish for them.

For not only will they study the technical details of their craft in this period of apprenticeship—they will learn also the habit of work without which the writer will never be more than an amateur. It is this habit of work which will bring the writer to his work table every day at the same hour, there to do about the same amount of work according to the capacity which experience tells him is naturally his. It is this habit of work which will teach him to

Source: *Reprinted by permission of Farrar, Straus and Giroux, Inc. Selection, adapted and abridged, from "Talking Shop" from* Approaches to Writing *by Paul Horgan. Copyright © by Paul Horgan.*

learn the hazardous and challenging necessity of keeping alive in his imagination a work of art which may take many months or even years to complete.

And here—since this discussion has entered the workroom—here is a parenthesis of shop-talk: a certain work of my own—a very long book—took ten years to complete. Every time I came to work on it day after day and year after year I had to draw conviction anew from the overall conception which brought me to respond to the project in the first place.

But there was more to this impulse of the initial conception than subject matter. One can be much taken by an idea, a place, a theme, and consider that it would make a fine book; but unless one's interest in the first notion is brought to projected form, it is probable that the idea itself will go the way of the hundreds of vague concepts which drift in and out of the writer's imagination without getting anywhere. There must then be two elements to insure the validity of a work about to be carried out. First, the initial impulse must have that inner sense of its plausibility which can defend itself against the myriad doubts which will assail it: those from within—the writer's own second thoughts and self-questionings; and those from without—those stray assaults upon the writer's current idea which come, all unintended in their damage, from chance remarks made by someone which can startle the writer with their applicability to his new subject, which might make it seem commonplace or unoriginal, or a line accidentally come upon in the writer's current reading which may seem to make trivial, or vulgar, or old hat, what he is nurturing in his thought. Many a potential work has been wrecked for the writer by just such idle hazards. In its inceptive stages a book is a vulnerable affair; it can be saved from extinction only if as early as possible it begins to find, in the writer's imagination, the precisely appropriate form for its fulfillment.

Once that is glimpsed, even incompletely, the subject, the idea, is safe; for in this combination of material and form, the initial energy of the work is preserved, and even through many years of composition, the writer can return daily to the next quota of his work with renewed belief in what he is doing. He is saved by the fact that the idea which first moved him is already enclosed in the design which he has found for its final presentation. If in the long haul the material momentarily seems to him to wear thin, or to have become over-familiar, he has now the beauty of his imagined form to renew him; and contemplating the whole each day as he works on the part, he is freshly empowered. Such has been my general experience. It has been this concern for a complete projection of the form, combined with the discipline of daily work, which has sustained me throughout.

Finally it is in this habit of work where the writer finds his real sense of achievement—his very content. He is really himself, at his best, only when he is observing his rhythm of work. If a day, or a week, or a month must go by when he does not work, he may think he is having a well-deserved rest; but he cannot deceive himself. He feels obscurely guilty. And if his period of inaction results from a temporary inability to work—if he is in one of those vacant phases between large productions—then he is in a state of acute misery, and he feels that hardly anything equals his joy when the day comes that will see him at work again.

Once he achieves a certain command of expression the writer must yield himself wholly to it. Illustrations are plentiful out of the lives of literary men. The yielding is not always agreeable; indeed, it is often tyrannical. Listen to Charles Dickens saying no to an importunate lady:

> *I hold my inventive capacity on the stern condition that it master my whole life, often have complete possession of me, make its own demands upon me, and sometimes, for months together, put everything else away from me . . . All this I can hardly expect you to understand—or the restlessness and waywardness of an author's mind . . . it is impossible to command one's self to any stipulated and set disposal of five minutes . . . the mere consciousness of an engagement will sometimes worry a whole day. These are the penalties paid for writing books. Whoever is devoted to an art must be content to deliver himself wholly up to it. I am grieved if you suspect me of not wanting to see you, but I can't help it; I must go my way whether or no.*

Some work with a stream-like fluency, some must dig every inch of the way. Flaubert wrote to George Sand,

> *You don't know what it is to stay a whole day with your head in your hands trying to squeeze your unfortunate brain so as to find a word. Ideas come very easily with you, incessantly, like a stream. With me it is a tiny thread of water. Hard labor at art is necessary for me before obtaining a waterfall. Ah! I certainly know the agonies of style.*

The point is, easy or hard, the work was done, and done only by incessant application.

My own habit brings me to my work table at about the same time every day—roughly at half-past nine. But actually, the working day starts earlier. It starts on awakening, with a sort of bated breath in the thought, if I may put it so. Preparation for the morning's task gets under way in an induced and protected absent-mindedness, as if to allow the work in progress to come clear gradually, so that its daily rebirth suffers no jarring collisions with immediate reality, but establishes its own reality from which it will draw conviction. Absurd as it may appear to those in other vocations, any contact with a serious distraction, or obligation elsewhere, may, at this daily moment, disturb a balance already delicate. A phone call is a minor catastrophe and a knock on the door a potential disaster. Until the day's work can actually begin, a frowning selfishness protects all the ingredients of plan, design, idea, and will; and when it begins, it flows forth, if the day is a good one, or it struggles forth, if it is a poor one; but strangely, later, it is difficult to tell by the evidence which pages came from fluent work and which from halting. It is again a reflection of the discipline we have mentioned.

Not everyone counts his pages against his clock like Trollope, who said he worked to produce two hundred fifty words every fifteen minutes in his allotted work time. This was an efficiency almost unearthly, and so was the calm technical virtuosity with which, according to the legend, he immediately began another novel when he finished his current one with a quarter of an hour to spare. A similar story was told of George Sand by the Goncourts in their *Journal*. "One day she finished a novel at one o'clock in the morning... and immediately started another"—this quoted from Louis Kronenberger's *The Pleasure of Their Company*.

Experience tells the writer what his proper daily quota of work should be. If he exceeds it at all appreciably, he probably finds that the quality of his work falls off, and that in consequence he must rewrite more than usual to make up for it. If the form of a piece of writing has been solved beforehand, rewriting of great blocks of work does not often follow. But revision word by word and sentence does follow, for me, not once, but many times, each for different values.

These embrace precision in meaning; as between two words of equal precision, choice, then, of that one which calls up image more vividly through color or sound or association; rhythm, the great key to readability, in small units of the text, such as the phrase and the sentence, rhythm in larger developments of the text, such as the paragraph and the chapter, and finally rhythm in the work as a whole. In fiction, revision pursues each character of the story in a separate reading to feel the consistency, the living presence of each. Another complete revision is devoted to an examination to improve atmosphere and background. And so on, paying attention to each of the elements, including the humble mechanics, which combine to make a finished work—such matters as simple correctness in spelling, puncuation, grammar, syntax—the technical fabric by which the rich English language, with all its tributaries, is given its primary power of communication.

The writings of many students would lead us to think such matters too trivial to engage the personal attention of a serious author. It is the rare student, even in the graduate school of letters, who can spell, or even cares about it, or who understands the purposes of punctuation, or dissects the sentence in order to learn its anatomy, or even rereads at least once to correct typographic errors. When I have begged students to spare me their acts of simple carelessness, and have assured them that an editor will pay little attention to a typescript whose early pages reveal a sustained illiteracy, I have been told many times by them that "the editor would put in the spelling, punctuation, et cetera."

And yet such elements as I speak of are the structural fibers of writing, and not to respect them for their own sake, and to love their purposes and their powers, is to have little promise as a writer. What would we think of a music student who disdained to master the C major scale because he preferred to think only about playing whole sonatas even with a thousand wrong notes? The illustration is not too fanciful, as any instructor in advanced writing can testify.

Leaving the comforts of the concrete, through which we have made common connection with the art and discipline of writing, we come to other aspects of the subject. We must go beyond pencil boxes, as it were, and look beyond the page, to consider the writer's vision of life which all simple and habitual mechanics of writing exist to serve. His worth as a writer will generally rest upon several values. He will be a writer worth reading according as:

—His vision is his own.

—His vision has the power to move him to repeated revelations of it, in whatever medium—poetry, the drama, history, the novel, the story, philosophy: in other words, if his vision is the source of abundance.

—His vision has a life-giving quality by which the minds and hearts of others are moved to their own expression in thought or act.

—His vision embraces a power of design so that not only the content but also the form of his work will create a second life out of his materials.

—His vision is complete: if it goes past the fashion of his time and the bias of current social or psychological attitude to seek out and share a sense of life's unity, and to find in it that memory of creation which seems to contain and account for all things.

Where many literary workers fall short of making significant works is just here where spiritual values come into focus in a point of view.

The spiritual life of the modern world becomes increasingly fragmented. Modern writers, like everybody else, long for a nourishing explanation of life; but all too many turn to recent and fugitive systems of imposing orderly but incomplete designs upon life's teeming and elusive variety, and in doing so, seem to lose the deepest well of their inspiration, and that is, their artistic intuition. Much of our writing now seems to be propped up by a foundation of earnest observation rather than by one of intuitive identity, or all-enduring, communion, with mankind.

To put it in another way, let us say that we are living in the age of the case history. Much of this century's admired creative literature seems to arise from clinical observation and theory rather than from a stroke of knowledge in heart and soul.

Clinical understanding of behavior has value in the practice of therapy. But literature and therapy have quite distinctly separate purposes, and to confuse the two is fatal for the artist. Behavioral patterns of society and individuals have been taken by many modern artists as their points of under-standing and departure for works of writing. But these are the stuff of science, which goes after truth and demonstrates it in a way wholly different from the artist's way. Diagnosis is not the same thing as creation and systematic com-prehension does not equal empathy. Many writers in our day have lost their true way by following a clinical approach to their commentaries upon life. They seem to promise verisimilitude, and to guarantee accuracy. They show us how people act—according to theoretical interpretations, which more often rob the represented figure of unique character than endow him with it. Some works emerging under such a system may have seemed to a wide public to open new ways of expression to the writer. I think it possible that the authors of such works have been intellectually seduced by psychological speculative-ness where they would better have been occupied with discovering their own best capacities to enter into human nature in their own unique terms as artists.

For systems of theoretical interpretation and schools of psychology change with the generations, and so offer only means of expression without a future. The very vocabularies of these systems are subject to fugitive fashion, as you may readily recognize if you turn in on the jargon of earlier systems of the study of life which were once taken seriously and considered perdurable. That which is based on an obedient and earnest observance of fashion must change too, and there we say goodbye to the wholeness of vision which we ask of our interpreters.

When aesthetic perception approaches its fullest realization, it is akin to man's religious vision, whatever form this may take. Faith is a supernatural grace. The true poet, the true artist, is he who knows without learning. His own intuition is closer to the supernatural than to any prevailing temper of the pluralistic and pragmatic modern culture.

Joyce Carol Oates is one of America's most prolific writers of stories, novels, poems, essays, and reviews. After attending Syracuse University and the University of Wisconsin, Oates planned to work toward a doctorate, but turned instead to writing full time when she was selected for the Honor Roll of *Best American Short Stories*. An outpouring of impressive work has followed, including *Wonderland* (a National Book Award Nominee in 1972), *Them* (1978), and *A Sentimental Education* (1981). Her fiction often reflects the turbulence of emotions and violence in contemporary America. "Reality," she has argued, "is always the foundation of art." After many years of teaching at the University of Windsor, Oates now serves on the faculty of Princeton University.

The Making of Fiction

Joyce Carol Oates

As a teacher of creative writing, as well as a writer, I am very deeply concerned with the phenomenon of "creativity"—it is one of the most mysterious of all human endeavors, and must ultimately be considered in the light of long-range evolutionary patterns in man. The process of creating art cannot be understood, cannot be explained in rational or scientific terms. Assistants of Einstein's at Princeton were often astonished at the apparent ease with which Einstein "thought" through problems that seemed opaque to them— he would pace slowly around his office, curling a lock of hair around a finger, his face quite abstract and gentle, showing no effort of concentration. Then after a few minutes he would smile happily—and the problem was solved. Though his assistants were grateful for his superior imagination, they were rather frustrated because they could not begin to comprehend the thought-processes that Einstein experienced; nor could he explain them. So in the end it is better not to attempt explanations, but to rejoice in this spontaneous and only partly-willed miracle of the imagination.

What writers can share with one another, however, is their knowledge of how the process can be stimulated and formalized into art. For, without the conscious and intelligent formalization of one's deepest, instinctive fantasies, no communication at all is possible. I think that post-Romantic, existentialist attitudes toward art—that it should be "spontaneous," that it should reflect a vital but intellectual reality—are quite erroneous, and present a dangerous temptation to writers who are not certain of themselves. Whenever a writer or philosopher or poet stresses the Unconscious, one should remember that it is not his "Unconscious" that is speaking, but his conscious mind. If Sartre's apparent judgment of man is that he is a "useless passion," one should ask whether Sartre himself seems to believe this—whether, in the light of his long, distinguished, dedicated career, his own writing can be considered "useless." We must never take writers at their own estimation of themselves or of us; probably we are all more complex and more noble, if we bother to examine ourselves.

Fiction and poetry celebrate the "unique"—what the writer has experienced or thought, personally; without this personal, private experience, the story or poem will be simply manufactured. One really cannot "manufacture" emotions. But there is no reason to make them up, since everyone has emotions—daydreams—unique and unrepeatable experiences. The important thing is, do people correctly value themselves? If they are writing, why are they writing? Anyone who is writing "to make money" is deluding himself; he is writing for other, deeper reasons, reasons he cannot explain. But as long as he believes that he is writing "for money" or "for prestige," he will write in a falsifying way, manufacturing emotions in conformity with emotions he sees in others; and yet his own life is filled with enough drama to constitute any number of novels. . . . When one writes about his true subject, in contrast to the usual "false" subject, he really has no difficulty with writing. But he must understand how his "unique" life is related to a vast "universal" life: the connection between the two is what he must write about.

I would be unable to write about anything that did not seem to me both unique and universal—an event I have lived through myself, or experienced intensely through my imagination, and an event that has some meaning, some larger appeal, which may go far beyond the temporal limitations of the subject. If art has any general evolutionary function, it must be to enhance the race, to work somehow toward an essential unity and harmony—survival and growth—and perhaps an integration of the human world with the natural world. The genesis for my novel, *Wonderland,* was a newspaper item I read years ago; it took a very long time for this to work its way through my imagination, and to emerge into consciousness, and the entire process is unknown to me. But the important thing, for me, is that the novel's basis is a real event; that it happened in the world "out there" and not in my head; that it must be sent back out into the world, and given a definite time and place, and related to current history.

Until this is settled I am unable to write and would not care to write—my own fantasies, however intriguing, simply don't seem substantial enough for me to formalize into art. I can sometimes "marry" them to objective events, since we all experience a number of the same things, and this allows me to write quite swiftly and happily; one of the large consolations for experiencing anything unpleasant is the knowledge that one can communicate it, especially one's triumph over it, to other people. Critics who chide me for dwelling on unpleasant and even bloody subjects miss the point: art shows us how to get through and transcend pain, and a close reading of any tragic work (*Macbeth* comes immediately to mind) will allow the intelligent reader to see how and why the tragedy took place, and how he, personally, need not make these mistakes. The more violent the murders in *Macbeth,* the more relief one can feel at not having to perform them. Great art is cathartic; it is always moral.

Therefore, one should contemplate his own experiences and see how they illuminate the experiences of others; how they transcend the finite; how they may be of value to other people. Unless there is a real "value," the resulting art will be manufactured and one-dimensional. I firmly believe that mankind is so instinctively, unconsciously involved with the survival and growth of the species that when an individual attempts to live *selfishly,* he will either fail or will fall into despair. Only when men are connected to larger, universal goals are they really happy—and one result of their happiness is a rush of creative activity. Any writer who has difficulty in writing is probably not onto his true subject, but wasting time with false, petty goals; as soon as you connect with your true subject you will write.

My purpose in writing this essay is to point out, I hope not dogmatically, that the average person is deeper, more talented, and more intelligent than he probably believes. He is transformable—even overnight. Exhaustion and fatigue are mainly psychological; if man is faced with a new challenge, he can summon up amazing reservoirs of energy. Unfortunately, our complex civilization reduces "challenges" for us or makes them seem apparently insoluble. It is the task of the writer to think his way through all the temporal, private, petty, headline-tormented confusion of his life, and connect with deeper rhythms, either through a conscious exploration of art, history, music, literature, or through personal discipline and meditation. Man is the only creature in possible control of his own destiny, and the most imaginative people will imagine their futures and the future of their society, not through being passive or influenced by current fashionable trends, but through a conscious exertion of the mind. If anyone who reads this is doubtful he should ask himself why he is doubtful; very likely he hasn't much idea of his own mind, and thinks himself far more limited than he really is.

On a more practical level—since writers are involved in the real world, for better or worse—I can offer only a few general advisory words, which may be too personal for broader application. My "ideas" come to me partly out of the world (I scan newspapers often) and partly out of my own life. They seem to sink into unconsciousness, sometimes for a long period of time, and are drawn out again by some stray reminder in my daily life (in the case of *Wonderland,* I came across a number of similar news items—dealing with the murder-suicide tragedy, eerily common in our country, in which a father kills his entire family and then himself). Then a long process of "dreaming-through" takes place, in which I think about the entire novel—living through various scenes, hearing or inventing dialogue, walking around with my characters in my head for months; only when the process is completed can I begin to write, and I can't hurry the process. I can assign to myself occasional tasks—how to manage a certain scene, how to dramatize the relationship of one character to another—before going to sleep at night, and sometimes by morning I have figured out the problem—sometimes—this might work about half the time. But I never despair or become impatient; it is simply a matter of waiting until the entire book is thought out. Of course, writing a short story is far easier. Henry James dictated his long, excellent story "The Beast in the Jungle" in *three mornings*—which suggests to me that he dreamt through his writing in great detail, before formalizing it.

After this strange, uncanny, intuitive stage of a novel is more or less completed in my mind, I write the first draft. I usually write very quickly, chapter by chapter, though I try to alternate work on a novel with shorter pieces—stories, articles, or reviews—in order to keep some objectivity. I always know exactly how the novel will end, even the wording of the final paragraph. I always know exactly the crucial scenes, the dialogue, even the way my characters look, though I may not describe them in that much detail. But as I write this first draft, I often discover new, small things about my characters, and allow any workable rearrangements in. This year, spent in London, I wrote a rather long novel titled *Do With Me What You Will,* which is a complex narrative dealing with the Law—the legal profession in America—but concentrating on two individuals who happen to be lovers, and who are married and "thinking back" over the circumstances of their having met and fallen in love; it involved many exasperating problems, but as long as I waited patiently the narrative always straightened out, and the characters asserted themselves in accordance with their own integrity.

After the first draft is finished, I put it aside temporarily and work on other things. Then, when I feel the time is come for me to really formalize it, I begin the second and final draft—and this part of the process is, strangely enough, the most enjoyable of all. I cut each chapter drastically, seeing as objectively as possible what can be eliminated or shortened (my manuscripts would be very long, sometimes twice as long, if I didn't cut so severely), trying to read the work as if from another part of myself, or from the point of view of another person. Though the original, spontaneous part of writing can be very exciting, the real reward for me at least is this third and most conscious, most "intellectual" organization of material. Man is a problem-solving animal, and the organizing of vast subjects must give pleasure, evidently; nothing seems to me to involve more intellectual effort than the organizing of a big novel, and I cannot imagine anything more rewarding.

In all this, I try to keep in mind the delicate relationship between what is unique, perhaps even eccentric, and what is universal—what will, hopefully, transcend the finite nature of newspaper headlines. Only in this relationship is there a true subject, worthy of long hours of work. I believe that all art is moral and that it must communicate either directly or through metaphor; I also believe that many people are true artists who imagine themselves only consumers, or at best only careful imitators of what seems marketable and timely.

Inspiration

There is such a thing as inspiration (lower case), but it is no miracle. It is the reward handed to a writer for hard work and good conduct. It is the felicitous words sliding, after hours of evasion, obediently into place. It is a sudden comprehension of how to manufacture an effect, finish off a line or a stanza. At the triumphant moment this gift may seem like magic, but actually it is the result of effort, practice, and the slight temperature a sulky brain is apt to run when it is pushed beyond its usual exertions.

Phyllis McGinley

William Stafford's first book grew out of his experience as a conscientious objector in World War II. Although he has taught at Lewis and Clark College since 1948, he has also fought forest fires for the U.S. Forest Service, worked in oil refineries, baled hay on farms in the great plains, and served in various capacities for several peace organizations. He speaks of his writing as part of a daily pattern when "during a quiet interval, without felt obligation to do other than find [his] way from impulse to impulse," he follows even the most "wavery hint." He is best known for *Traveling Through the Dark* (1962), a collection of poems that won both the National Book Award and the Shelley Memorial Award. In addition to Danforth and Guggenheim Fellowships, he has served as Consultant in Poetry to the Library of Congress. His most recent collection of poems, *Stories That Could Be True,* was published in 1977.

A Way of Writing

William Stafford

A writer is not so much someone who has something to say as he is someone who has found a process that will bring about new things he would not have thought of if he had not started to say them. That is, he does not draw on a reservoir; instead, he engages in an activity that brings to him a whole succession of unforeseen stories, poems, essays, plays, laws, philosophies, religions, or—but wait!

Back in school, from the first when I began to try to write things, I felt this richness. One thing would lead to another; the world would give and give. Now, after twenty years or so of trying, I live by that certain richness, an idea hard to pin, difficult to say, and perhaps offensive to some. For there are strange implications in it.

One implication is the importance of just plain receptivity. When I write, I like to have an interval before me when I am not likely to be interrupted. For me, this means usually the early morning, before others are awake. I get pen and paper, take a glance out of the window (often it is dark out there), and wait. It is like fishing. But I do not wait very long, for there is always a nibble—and this is where receptivity comes in. To get started I will accept

Source: From Writing The Australian Crawl by William Stafford. Copyright © by The University of Michigan, 1978. Reprinted by permission of the University of Michigan Press.

anything that occurs to me. Something always occurs, of course, to any of us. We can't keep from thinking. Maybe I have to settle for an immediate impression: it's cold, or hot, or dark, or bright, or in between! Or—well, the possibilities are endless. If I put down something, that thing will help the next thing come, and I'm off. If I let the process go on, things will occur to me that were not at all in my mind when I started. These things, odd or trivial as they may be, are somehow connected. And if I let them string out, surprising things will happen.

If I let them string out.... Along with initial receptivity, then, there is another readiness: I must be willing to fail. If I am to keep on writing, I cannot bother to insist on high standards. I must get into action and not let anything stop me, or even slow me much. By "standards" I do not mean "correctness"—spelling, punctuation, and so on. These details become mechanical for anyone who writes for a while. I am thinking about such matters as social significance, positive values, consistency, etc. I resolutely disregard these. Something better, greater, is happening! I am following a process that leads so wildly and originally into new territory that no judgment can at the moment be made about values, significance, and so on. I am making something new, something that has not been judged before. Later others—and maybe I myself—will make judgments. Now, I am headlong to discover. Any distraction may harm the creating.

So, receptive, careless of failure, I spin out things on the page. And a wonderful freedom comes. If something occurs to me, it is all right to accept it. It has one justification: it occurs to me. No one else can guide me. I must follow my own weak, wandering, diffident impulses.

A strange bonus happens. At times, without my insisting on it, my writings become coherent; the successive elements that occur to me are clearly related. They lead by themselves to new connections. Sometimes the language, even the syllables that happen along, may start a trend. Sometimes the materials alert me to something waiting in my mind, ready for sustained attention. At such times, I allow myself to be eloquent, or intentional, or for great swoops (Treacherous! Not to be trusted!) reasonable. But I do not insist on any of that; for I know that back of my activity there will be the coherence of my self, and that indulgence of my impulses will bring recurrent patterns and meanings again.

This attitude toward the process of writing creatively suggests a problem for me, in terms of what others say. They talk about "skills" in writing. Without denying that I do have experience, wide reading, automatic orthodoxies and maneuvers of various kinds, I still must insist that I am often baffled about what "skill" has to do with the precious little area of confusion when I do not know what I am going to say and then I find out what I am going to say. That precious interval I am unable to bridge by skill. What can I witness about it? It remains mysterious, just as all of us must feel puzzled about how we are so inventive as to be able to talk along through complexities with our friends, not needing to plan what we are going to say, but never stalled for long in our confident forward progress. Skill? If so, it is the skill we all have, something we must have learned before the age of three or four.

A writer is one who has become accustomed to trusting that grace, or luck, or—skill.

Yet another attitude I find necessary: most of what I write, like most of what I say in casual conversation, will not amount to much. Even I will realize, and even at the time, that it is not negotiable. It will be like practice. In conversation I allow myself random remarks—in fact, as I recall, that is the way I learned to talk—so in writing I launch many expendable efforts. A result of this free way of writing is that I am not writing for others, mostly; they will not see the product at all unless the activity eventuates in something that later appears to be worthy. My guide is the self, and its adventuring in the language brings about communication.

This process-rather-than-substance view of writing invites a final, dual reflection:

1. Writers may not be special—sensitive or talented in any usual sense. They are simply engaged in sustained use of a language skill we all have. Their "creations" come about through confident reliance on stray impulses that will, with trust, find occasional patterns that are satisfying.

2. But writing itself is one of the great, free human activities. There is scope for individuality, and elation, and discovery, in writing. For the person who follows with trust and forgiveness what occurs to him, the world remains always ready and deep, an inexhaustible environment, with the combined vividness of an actuality and flexibility of a dream. Working back and forth between experience and thought, writers have more than space and time can offer. They have the whole unexplored realm of human vision.

Richard Hugo was educated at the University of Washington and worked for Boeing Company in Seattle for twelve years before his poetry began to be recognized. Since then he has published twelve volumes of poetry and been twice nominated for the National Book Award. *What Thou Lovest Well Remains American* (1975) received the Theodore Roethke Memorial Award; his *Selected Poems* (1979) was runner-up for the Pulitzer Prize in 1980. Other honors include a Guggenheim Fellowship that led to his most recent volume, *The Right Madness on Skye* (1980), about which poet Dave Smith has said, "Hugo gives us the chance to begin again and a world where that beginning is ever possible." Hugo is currently Director of the Creative Writing Program at the University of Montana and editor of the Yale Series of Younger Poets. His first novel, *Death and the Good Life,* was published in 1981.

Writing off the Subject

Richard Hugo

I often make these remarks to a beginning poetry-writing class.

You'll never be a poet until you realize that everything I say today and this quarter is wrong. It may be right for me, but it is wrong for you. Every moment, I am, without wanting or trying to, telling you to write like me. But I hope you learn to write like you. In a sense, I hope I don't teach you how to write but how to teach yourself how to write. At all times keep your crap detector on. If I say something that helps, good. If what I say is of no help, let it go. Don't start arguments. They are futile and take us away from our purpose. As Yeats noted, your important arguments are with yourself. If you don't agree with me, don't listen. Think about something else.

When you start to write, you carry to the page one of two attitudes, though you may not be aware of it. One is that all music must conform to truth. The other, that all truth must conform to music. If you believe the first, you are making your job very difficult, and you are not only limiting the writing of poems to something done only by the very witty and clever, such as Auden, you are weakening the justification for creative-writing programs.

Source: *"Writing Off the Subject" is reprinted from* The Triggering Town, Lectures and Essays on Poetry and Writing, *by Richard Hugo, by permission of W. W. Norton & Company, Inc. Copyright ©* 1979 *by W. W. Norton & Company, Inc.*

So you can take that attitude if you want, but you are jeopardizing my livelihood as well as your chances of writing a good poem.

If the second attitude is right, then I still have a job. Let's pretend it is right because I need the money. Besides, if you feel truth must conform to music, those of us who find life bewildering and who don't know what things mean, but love the sounds of words enough to fight through draft after draft of a poem, can go on writing—try to stop us.

One mark of a beginner is his impulse to push language around to make it accommodate what he has already conceived to be the truth, or, in some cases, what he has already conceived to be the form. Even Auden, clever enough at times to make music conform to truth, was fond of quoting the woman in the Forster novel who said something like, "How do I know what I think until I see what I've said."

A poem can be said to have two subjects, the initiating or triggering subject, which starts the poem or "causes" the poem to be written, and the real or generated subject, which the poem comes to say or mean, and which is generated or discovered in the poem during the writing. That's not quite right because it suggests that the poet recognizes the real subject. The poet may not be aware of what the real subject is but only have some instinctive feeling that the poem is done.

Young poets find it difficult to free themselves from the initiating subject. The poet puts down the title: "Autumn Rain." He finds two or three good lines about Autumn Rain. Then things start to break down. He cannot find anything more to say about Autumn Rain so he starts making up things, he strains, he goes abstract, he starts telling us the meaning of what he has already said. The mistake he is making, of course, is that he feels obligated to go on talking about Autumn Rain, because that, he feels, is the subject. Well, it isn't the subject. You don't know what the subject is, and the moment you run out of things to say about Autumn Rain start talking about something else. In fact, it's a good idea to talk about something else before you run out of things to say about Autumn Rain.

Don't be afraid to jump ahead. There are a few people who become more interesting the longer they stay on a single subject. But most people are like me, I find. The longer they talk about one subject, the duller they get. Make the subject of the next sentence different from the subject of the sentence you just put down. Depend on rhythm, tonality, and the music of language to hold things together. It is impossible to write meaningless sequences. In a sense the next thing always belongs. In the world of imagination, all things belong. If you take that on faith, you may be foolish, but foolish like a trout.

Never worry about the reader, what the reader can understand. When you are writing, glance over your shoulder, and you'll find there is no reader. Just you and the page. Feel lonely? Good. Assuming you can write clear English sentences, give up all worry about communication. If you want to communicate, use the telephone.

To write a poem you must have a streak of arrogance—not in real life I hope. In real life try to be nice. It will save you a hell of a lot of trouble and give you more time to write. By arrogance I mean that when you are writing you must assume that the next thing you put down belongs not for reasons of logic, good sense, or narrative development, but because you put it there. You, the same person who said that, also said this. The adhesive force is your way of writing, not sensible connection.

The question is: how to get off the subject, I mean the triggering subject. One way is to use words for the sake of their sounds. Later, I'll demonstrate this idea.

The initiating subject should trigger the imagination as well as the poem. If it doesn't, it may not be a valid subject but only something you feel you should write a poem about. Never write a poem about anything that ought to have a poem written about it, a wise man once told me. Not bad advice but not quite right. The point is, the triggering subject should not carry with it moral or social obligations to feel or claim you feel certain ways. If you feel pressure to say what you know others want to hear and don't have enough devil in you to surprise them, shut up. But the advice is still well taken. Subjects that ought to have poems have a bad habit of wanting lots of other things at the same time. And you provide those things at the expense of your imagination.

I suspect that the true or valid triggering subject is one in which physical characteristics or details correspond to attitudes the poet has toward the world and himself. For me, a small town that has seen better days often works. Contrary to what reviewers and critics say about my work, I know almost nothing of substance about the places that trigger my poems. Knowing can be a limiting thing. If the population of a town is nineteen but the poem needs the sound seventeen, seventeen is easier to say if you don't know the population. Guessing leaves you more options. Often, a place that starts a poem for me is one I have only glimpsed while passing through. It should make impression enough that I can see things in the town—the water tower, the bank, the last movie announced on the marquee before the theater shut down for good, the closed hotel—long after I've left. Sometimes these are imagined things I find if I go back, but real or imagined, they act as a set of stable knowns that sit outside the poem. They and the town serve as a base of operations for the poem. Sometimes they serve as a stage setting. I would never try to locate a serious poem in a place where physical evidence suggests that the people there find it relatively easy to accept themselves—say the new Hilton.

The poet's relation to the triggering subject should never be as strong as (must be weaker than) his relation to his words. The words should not serve the subject. The subject should serve the words. This may mean violating the facts. For example, if the poem needs the word "black" at some point and the grain elevator is yellow, the grain elevator may have to be black in the poem. You owe reality nothing and the truth about your feelings everything.

Let's take what I think is a lovely little poem, written in 1929 by a fine poet who has been unjustly ignored.

RATTLESNAKE

I found him sleepy in the heat
And dust of a gopher burrow,
Coiled in loose folds upon silence
In a pit of the noonday hillside.
I saw the wedged bulge
Of the head hard as a fist.
I remembered his delicate ways:
The mouth a cat's mouth yawning.
I crushed him deep in dust,
And heard the loud seethe of life
In the dead beads of the tail
Fade, as wind fades
*From the wild grain of the hill.**

I find there's much to be learned about writing from this excellent poem. First I think it demonstrates certain truths that hold for much art. The poem grows from an experience, either real or imagined—I only recently found out that this particular experience was real. The starting point is fixed to give the mind an operating base, and the mind expands from there. Often, if the triggering subject is big (love, death, faith) rather than localized and finite, the mind tends to shrink. Sir Alexander Fleming observed some mold, and a few years later we had a cure for gonorrhea. But what if the British government had told him to find a cure for gonorrhea? He might have worried so much he would not have noticed the mold. Think small. If you have a big mind, that will show itself. If you can't think small, try philosophy or social criticism.

The need for the poem to have been written is evident in the poem. This is a strong example of the notion that all good serious poems are born in obsession. Without this poem the experience would have been neither validated nor completed.

The poem has elements of melodrama. All art that has endured has a quality we call schmaltz or corn. Our reaction against the sentimentality embodied in Victorian and post-Victorian writing was so resolute writers came to believe that the further from sentimentality we got, the truer the art. That was a mistake. As Bill Kittredge, my colleague who teaches fiction writing, has

---

*Reprinted by permission of Brewster Ghiselin; first published in *Poetry* © 1939; reprinted in *Windrose Poems 1929–1979*, University of Utah Press, 1980.

pointed out: if you are not *risking* sentimentality, you are not close to your inner self.

The poem is located in a specific place. You don't know where, but you know the poet knows where. Knowing where you are can be a source of creative stability. If you are in Chicago you can go to Rome. If you ain't no place you can't go nowhere.

The snake is killed gratuitously. The study of modern psychology may have helped some of us become better people. We may treat our children better because we have gained some rudimentary notion of cause and effect in behavior. But in art, as seemingly in life, things happen without cause. They just happen. A poem seldom finds room for explanations, motivations, or reason. What if the poem read

> *Because I knew his poison*
> *Was dangerous to children*
> *I crushed him deep in dust . . . ?*

The poet would be making excuses for himself, and the fierce honesty with which he faces his raw act of murder would be compromised. Nothing in the drama *King Lear* can possibly serve as explanation of the shattering cruelty of Regan and Cornwall when they blind Gloucester. From a writer's standpoint, a good explanation is that Shakespeare knew a lot of creeps walk this earth.

But there's more to be learned from this poem than just artistic principles. They are always suspect anyway, including those I think I find here. Let's move on to the language of the poem.

Generally, in English multisyllabic words have a way of softening the impact of language. With multisyllabic words we can show compassion, tenderness, and tranquillity. With multisyllabic words we become more civilized. In the first four lines of the poem, seven of the twenty-six words, slightly better than one out of four, are two-syllable words. This is a fairly high count unless you are in politics. The snake is sleepy. He presents no threat to the speaker. His dwelling is that of a harmless creature, a gopher. It's almost as if the snake were a derelict, an orphan, a vagabond who sleeps wherever he can. The words "noonday hillside" suggest that the world does not have rigid topography but optional configurations. At 4 P.M. it might not be a hillside at all. We take our identities from our relationships, just as the earth takes its configurations from the time of day, the position of the source of light. This is a warm, fluid world.

With single-syllable words we can show rigidity, honesty, toughness, relentlessness, the world of harm unvarnished. In lines five and six, the snake is seen as a threat, the lines slam home heavy as the fist the poet sees as simile for the head of the snake. But of course, men, not snakes, have fists, and so we might ask: where does the danger really lie here?

The speaker then has a tender memory of the snake in lines seven and eight, and we get two three-syllable words and a long two-syllable word, "yawning." You might note that the poet is receptive to physical similarities of snakes and domestic cats—they look much alike when yawning—just as later he sees and hears the similarity of rattlesnakes to wheat (grain), the way the tail looks like the tassle, the way the rattle sounds like wind in the grain.

In the final five lines the poet kills the snake, faces himself and the moral implications of his act without a flinch or excuse, and we get no multisyllabic words in the entire passage. All single-syllable words, and the gaze is level, the whole being of the speaker honestly laid out, vulnerable on his private moral block. If one acts on the rigid prejudicial attitudes expressed in lines five and six (which the speaker did), and not on the fluid, tender, humane attitudes expressed in the first four lines and lines seven and eight, then in return one is faced with the fully developed, uncompromising picture of what one has done. Forever.

In this poem the triggering subject remains fully in view until late in the poem, whereas the generated object, what the poem is saying, just begins to show at the end but is nonetheless evident. The snake as such is being left behind, and attitudes about life are starting to form. The single-syllable words in the last five lines relentlessly drive home the conviction that all life is related, and that even if life isn't sacred, we might be better off if we acted as if it were. In this case the poet got off the initiating subject late.

I mentioned that one way of getting off the subject, of freeing yourself from memory if you will, is to use words for the sake of sound. Now I must use four lines from an early poem of mine, simply because I can't verify any other poet's process. I know what mine was at the time. These are the first four lines of the fourth stanza of an early poem called "At the Stilli's Mouth."

> With the Stilli this defeated and the sea
> turned slough by close Camano, how can water die
> with drama, in a final rich cascade,
> a suicide, a victim of terrain, a martyr?

When I was a young poet I set an arbitrary rule that when I made a sound I felt was strong, a sound I liked specially, I'd make a similar sound three to eight syllables later. Of course it would often be a slant rhyme. Why three to eight? Don't ask. You have to be silly to write poems at all.

In this case the word "cascade" fell lovingly on my ear and so, soon after, "suicide." I wasn't smart enough to know that I was saying that my need to see things dramatically was both childish and authentic. But "suicide" was right and led to "victim of terrain" and "martyr," associative notions at least, but also words that sound like other words in the passage, "martyr" like "drama" and "water," "victim" like "final" and "Stilli" (Northwest colloquial for Stilliguamish, the river). Instead of "suicide" I might have hit on "masquerade," but that would have been wrong and I hope I would have known it. I might have simply because "masquerade" sound *too much* like "cascade," calls attention to itself, and to my ear is less interesting. What I'm trying to tell you is that by doing things like this I was able to get off the subject and write the poem. The fact that "suicide" sounds like "cascade" is infinitely more important than what is being said.

It isn't of course, but if you think about it that way for the next twenty-five years you could be in pretty good shape.

Denise Levertov   has written over twenty books of poetry, essays, and poetry translations. Her father was a Russian Jew who became an Anglican minister in England. Levertov describes her childhood as a world of refugees, evacuees, exiles, and dancers. Privately educated by tutors, and with no formal college experience, she has gone on to teach at Drew University, Tufts, M.I.T., City College of New York, Vassar, and Berkeley. Her many awards include a Guggenheim in 1962 and the Boulton Prize in 1964. *Jacob's Ladder* (1961), *O Taste and See* (1964), and *Collected Earlier Poems* (1979) are among her best known works. "Work and Inspiration" is taken from a talk given at the Radcliffe Institute for Independent Study and later published in *The Poet in the World* (1960), her first book of prose essays.

Work and Inspiration: Inviting the Muse

Denise Levertov

Poems come into being in two ways. There are those which are—or used to be—spoken of as *inspired*; poems which seem to appear out of nowhere, complete or very nearly so; which are quickly written without conscious premeditation, taking the writer by surprise. These are often the best poems; at least, a large proportion of those that *I* have been "given" in this way are the poems I myself prefer and which readers, without knowledge of their history, have singled out for praise. Such poems often seem to have that aura of authority, of the incontrovertible, that air of being mysteriously lit from within their substance, which is exactly what a poet strives to attain in the poems that are hard to write. But though the inspired poem is something any poet naturally feels awed by and grateful for, nevertheless if one wrote only such poems one would have, as it were, no occupation; and so most writers, surely, are glad that some of their work requires the labor for which they are constitutionally fitted. For the artist—every kind of artist, and, I feel sure, not only the artist but everyone engaged in any kind of creative activity—is as enamored of the process of making as of the thing made.

There is nothing one can say directly concerning the coming into being of "given" of "inspired" poems, because there is no conscious process to be described. However, in considering what happens in writing poems which have a known history, I have come to feel convinced that they are not of a radically different order; it is simply that in the "given" poem *the same kind of work* has gone on below, or I would prefer to say beyond, the threshold of consciousness. The labor we call conscious is, if the poem is a good one, or rather if the poet knows how to work, not a matter of a use of the intellect divorced from other factors but of the intuitive interplay of various mental and physical factors, just as in unconscious precreative activity; it is *conscious* in that we are aware of it, but not in the sense of being deliberate and controlled by the rational will (though of course reason and will can and should play their modest part too).

The two manifestations of this underlyingly identical process can both occur in the composition of a single poem. Either sections of a poem emerge "right" the first time, while other sections require much revision; or, as I hope to demonstrate, many drafts and revisions can prepare the way for a poem which at the last leaps from the pen and requires little or no revision, but which is emphatically not simply a final draft and indeed bears practically no resemblance to the earlier "versions" which make it possible. In such a case conscious work has led to the unpredictable inspiration.

I have chosen to tell the history of three poems from *The Sorrow Dance*— "The Son," I and II, and "A Man"—as examples of what happens, of how the laboriously written poem evolves and how the labor can sometimes lead to the entire "given" poem. The choice of these particular poems was determined by my happening to have kept all the worksheets for them and also by the fact of their close connection with each other.

The first of the three to be written was the first "Son" poem. The earliest note for it says simply, "Nik as a presence, *Who he was.*" This was a reference to an unpublished poem written almost seventeen years before—in the spring of 1949, just before the birth of my son. I did not publish this poem, because I came to feel it was too wordy, just not good enough; but I shall quote it now as part of the story of these later poems:

> *One is already here whose life*
> *bearing like seed its distant death, shall grow*
> *through human pain, human joy, shall know*
> *music and weeping, only because*
> *the strange flower of your thighs*
> *bloomed in my body. From our joy*
> *begins a stranger's history. Who*
> *is this rider in the dark? We lie*
> *in candlelight; the child's quick unseen movements*
> *jerk my belly under your hand. Who,*
> *conceived in joy, in joy,*
> *lies nine months alone in a walled silence?*

Who is this rider in the dark
nine months the body's tyrant
nine months alone in a walled silence
our minds cannot fathom?
Who is it will come out of the dark,
whose cries demand our mercy, tyrant
no longer, but alone still, in a solitude
memory cannot reach?
Whose lips will suckle at these breasts,
thirsting, unafraid, for life?
Whose eyes will look out of that solitude?

The wise face of the unborn
ancient and innocent
must change to infant ignorance
before we see it, irrevocable third
looking into our lives; the child
must hunger, sleep, cry, gaze, long weeks
before it learns of laughter. Love can never
wish a life no darkness; but may love
be constant in the life our love has made.

My note saying *"Who he was"* referred to my memory of this poem, but I had not actually read the poem in several years, so it is to its general sense of questioning rather than to the specific words of the poem that I was harking back.

Next on the same piece of paper is the note, *"M.'s fineness of face—the lines—the changes out of boy-and-young-manhood. A life."* Out of these notes all three poems emerged.

The first draft of the first poem went like this:

He-who-came-forth was
it turned out
a man.

Through his childhood swiftly
ran the current of
pain, that men

communicate or lie,
the intelligence behind silence
not always heard.

In hyphenating "He-who-came-forth," making these words into a name or title, I think I may have had American Indian names obscurely in mind, and with them the knowledge that in some cultures a true name is gained only after initiation; and that some Indians achieved identity only after the Big Dream which established their special relation to life. I may also have had sounding in me the echo of a poem of Robert Duncan's, in which he writes: "Wanderer-To-Come-To-The-Secret-Place-Where-Waits-The-Discovery-That-Moves-The-Heart," (from "The Performance We Wait For" in *The Opening of the Field*).

In the second draft the first stanza remained, as indeed it continued to do throughout, unchanged, but I seem to have felt a need to elaborate the image of the current running through childhood, the current of knowledge of the human condition, that men communicate or lie, or one could say, communicate or die (or as Auden put it, "We must love one another or die"), but that this communication, which at times has to fight its way through silence, is a hard, hard task. But though my intention was to make this clearer, I only got so far as to elaborate on the brevity of childhood:

> *Childhood is very short*
> *and shot through hastily with*
> *gleams of that current*
>
> *straining to its . . .*

This was obviously impossible; the words themselves were straining; instead of waiting in that intense passivity, that passive intensity, that passionate patience which Keats named Negative Capability and which I believe to be a vital condition for the emergence of a true poem, I was straining to *find words*; the word had not found *me*. The word "straining," however, led me to my third try, where, again preceded by the unchanged first stanza,

> *He-who-came-forth was*
> *it turned out*
> *a man,*

I continued:

> *living among us*
> *his childhood sifted, strained out*
> *to retain*
>
> *all it held of*
> *pain, energy, lassitude,*
> *the imagination of man*

Here the last words were intended to lead into another attempt at giving a sense of that knowledge of the human condition, the seed in the child of adulthood, of manhood, which I had tried to speak of in the first draft. Again it was abandoned, with the continuing sense that the words were not the right words. The fourth draft begins to pick up a more concrete sense of the presence being talked of, *how* he lives among us:

> *Moving among us from room to room of*
> the soul's dark cottage
> *in boots, in jeans, in a cloak of flame no-one*
> *seems to see—*
>
> *it is*
> *the imagination's garment, that human dress*
> *women of fire and seagrasses—*
>
> *how swift the current was,*
> *'childhood,' that carried him here—*

In this version appear details that immediately asserted themselves to me as vivid and necessary and were retained—"in boots, in jeans, in a cloak of flame"—but also an allusion I later felt was extraneous, to "The soul's dark cottage," a quote from the seventeenth-century poet Edmund Waller's wonderful couplet which I have loved since childhood: "The soul's dark cottage, batter'd and decay'd,/Lets in new light through chinks which Time hath made." Also in this fourth draft the current, which in the beginning had been the current of pain running through childhood, becomes itself the current of childhood, and the brevity of childhood is expressed as the swiftness of that current. A variant of this draft says:

> *How swiftly childhood's*
> *little river carried him here!*

and pain—or knowledge of pain, knowledge of suffering—is spoken of in an image quickly abandoned as seeming sentimental:

> *an injured dragonfly*
> *cupped in his large gentle hands*

In retrospect, I don't think this documentary image is *in itself* sentimental; but it has the effect of sentimentality in this context because it is digressive and does not bring the occasion alluded to directly enough into the poem, letting it remain an allusion. Of equal importance in the immediate decision to strike it out was the sonically awkward juxtaposition of "injured" and "gentle." I tried the substitution of "tender" for "gentle"—an injured dragonfly cupped "tenderly"—but no, the whole thing was going off on a tack much too soft and pretty for what I wanted.

At this point I tried to get back to the human knowledge:

> *Man, whose imagination is not*
> *intuition, whose innocence*
> *cannot brace itself for the event*
> *but is gone*
> *over the edge, spared*
> *no twist of joy's knife, never*
> *missing a trick of pain*

I was disgusted here with what seemed to me a cheap attempt to use these well-worn idioms; I felt it was gimmicky.

In the fifth draft I went back to the river image:

> *How swiftly the little river of childhood*
> *carried him here, a current doubling back*
> *on its eddies only as the embroidery of a theme,*
> *a life's introduction and allegro!*
>
> *Already heavy with knowledge of*
> *speech and silence,*
> *human perhaps to the point of excess,*
> *of genius—*
> *to suffer and to imagine*

This version was abandoned because the musical allusion was, once more, a digression, an irrelevancy. In my sixth draft I went back yet again to write out all I had so far that seemed solid and right: the first stanza, "He-who-came-forth," and the second, which now changed to:

> *Moves among us from room to room of our life*

instead of "the soul's dark cottage," and from which the "cloak of flame" I had spoken of him wearing, along with boots and jeans, was now elaborated as:

> *This mantle, folded in him throughout*
> *that time called childhood (which is*
> *a little river, but swift) flared out, one ordinary day,*
> *to surround him—*
>
> *—pulled out of his pocket along with*
> *old candy wrappers*
> *a cloak*
> *whose fire feathers are*
> *suffering, passion, knowledge of speech,*
> *knowledge of silence . . .*

Now here, with the becoming aware of those old candy wrappers, I believe I was on the right track, but I didn't know it, for in a seventh draft I went back partially to "the soul's dark cottage":

Little shafts of day
pierce the chinks in our dwelling.
He-who-came-forth
moves across them
trailing fire-feathers. Slowly.

In the eighth draft the flame enwrapping him becomes a *fine* flame, and those shafts of light coming through the chinks become first "the harsh light we live in" and then "common light." I was getting close to a resolution. This process had been going on for some days by this time, and in order not to confuse you too hopelessly I have omitted reference to a number of variant words in some drafts. The eighth, and as it proved, final version, took place, as it had to, in a state where without further effort the elements I now had on hand seemed to regroup themselves, and the concrete evidence of the thing finally *seen,* instead of strained after, entered the picture. In this final draft I got back to my established particulars and was led, from the candy wrappers, to see the curls of dust that gather in the corners of pockets, and to realize how treasures are transferred from one garment to another—and this cloak of flame was after all a treasure. Instead of any disquisition on the nature of the cloak of flame, I now felt I could depend on the context to imply this; that is, it is stated right away that He-who-came-forth has turned out to be a man, yet the jeans and boots and candy wrappers suggest youth; and though the cloak of flame is something he has had from the beginning, it is only now that it is unfurled. The fact that "no one seems to see it" is modified to "almost unseen in common light"—have you ever looked at a candle flame in hard morning light, almost invisible? I now had a poem that seemed complete in itself though reduced from my original intentions—or rather, my dim sense of its possible scope; and some of my sense of its being complete came from my recognition of its sonic structure, the way certain unifying sounds had entered it: the *m* of *man* leading directly to the *m* of *moves, flame* echoing in *lain,* and the *err* sounds of *wrappers, transferred, curl, unfurled,* which bind the center of the poem, actually unfurling in the *f*'s, open *a, s*'s, *t*'s, and *i*'s of the last two lines.

THE SON

i The Disclosure

He-who-came-forth was
it turned out
a man—

*Moves among us from room to room of our life
in boots, in jeans, in a cloak of flame
pulled out of his pocket along with
old candywrappers, where it had lain
transferred from pants to pants,
folded small as a curl of dust,
from the beginning—*

unfurled now.

*The fine flame
almost unseen in common light.**

Yet, in trusting that the image of the cloak of flame would pull its own weight though unqualified, unsupported, and would imply its meaning as a human and personal potential coming into play, I had cut too drastically from the poem any sense of the capacity for suffering inherent in this potential. I was eventually to come to the second "Son" poem by way of a realization of this lack. But meanwhile, something familiar but always exhilarating occurred; the wave of energy which had built up during the writing of one poem led me directly into another. The note about the lines on a face and "A life," written on the same piece of paper as "Who he was" but referring to a man in the middle of life, was mnemonic for a complex of feelings I had long been carrying.

My first try at this poem was dull and explanatory:

*A man dreams and
interprets his dreams
A man makes
fictions, but he passes
from making fictions on into
knowledge, into
laughter and grief.*

And in the margin I wrote, "The dreams of animals pass uninterpreted." This was just an attempt to warm up, a casting about for a clue. The second draft began by picking up from it:

*A Man is what
imagines the world, imagines
what imagines the world.
He can weep*

---

*"The Son I," by Denise Levertov, from *The Sorrow Dance*. Copyright © 1965 by Denise Levertov. Reprinted by permission of New Directions.

> *for not having wept,*
> *he laughs*
> *helplessly at what is not, it is*
> *so funny.*

But then this draft got involved in an irrelevant conceit:

> Seven long years ago
> they stole little Bridget—
> *thy soul, man! O,*
> *what deep lines*
> *are dug in thy cheeks*
> *by all She has undergone,*
> *and you standing*
> *so still, you thought,*
> *on the one spot those*
> *seven minutes!*

What had happened here was that certain troubles had occurred seven years before in the life of the man I was writing about, and their repercussions had continued ever since; this made me think both of the seven-year units of biological growth and change of which I had read, and of the mythological importance of the number seven. Seven years and a day is often the period of trial in fairy tales; Thomas the Rhymer found he had passed seven years in Elfland when he thought it was but a day; and in the poem by William Allingham, a nineteenth-century Irish poet, which I had quoted, or rather misquoted, little Bridget is stolen by the fairies for seven years. My conceit identified her with the soul, and tried to convey the idea that the soul's experiences, even those that remain unconscious, mark the face with expressive lines, though the consciousness may suppose that no change and development have been taking place. Both the conscious and unconscious living of the inner life, *living* it and not denying it, are essential to human value and dignity; yet we undervalue the inner life at times when the outer life of action and achievement does not synchronize with it; so that the man of whom I was writing had spoken of himself in anguish as having been at a standstill for seven years, because his outer life seemed baffled. The last lines of this draft:

> *How fair the dark*
> *of thy deep look is,*
> *the beauty*
> *of thy being*
> *a man!*

comment on the visible effects of inner experience, trying to say that the endurance of suffering, the acceptance of the trials of the soul, even though the life of action in the external world seems at a standstill, is what gives a man his human beauty.

Feeling that the introduction of legend seemed (though in fact it happened naturally) too recherché, especially since when Bridget returns to the world she cannot live there but dies of sorrow at all that has changed during her absence, my third draft of this poem tried to be more direct but was only prosy:

> *'Living a life' is what gives*
> *the beauty of deep lines*
> *dug in your cheeks*
>
> *Not what you have done but*
> *what seven years and seven*
> *or seven again gather*
> *in your eyes, in the*

And at that point the poem was put aside for a day or so; I felt baffled and dejected. But in this period of rest, or at least of inaction, the force of creative intuition had a chance to take over. All the explicit elements I have mentioned retired into some quiet place in my mind; and what emerged, complete save for a single word, was the poem "A Man" as it now stands.

A MAN

> *'Living a life'—*
> *the beauty of deep lines*
> *dug in your cheeks.*
>
> *The years gather by sevens*
> *to fashion you. They are blind,*
> *but you are not blind.*
>
> *Their blows resound,*
> *they are deaf, those laboring*
> *daughters of the Fates,*
>
> *but you are not deaf,*
> *you pick out*
> *your own song from the uproar*
>
> *line by line,*
> *and at last throw back*
> *your head and sing it.**

*"A Man," by Denise Levertov, from *The Sorrow Dance*. Copyright © 1965 by Denise Levertov. Reprinted by permission of New Directions.

Instead of the alien presence of Little Bridget, instead of abstract references to seven-year units, I was given a vision of "the years" embodied as figures that I think are at once more personal and more universal. The facts about them revealed themselves as I envisioned them—their blindness, their deafness, their brutal laboring persistence. In the third stanza I first wrote them down as "craftsmen," but I looked again and saw they were female figures, resembling the fates, the norns, and also the muses;† and then I suddenly knew that they were not the fates themselves but the years, the daughters of the fates. When the vision is given one, one has only to record. And with visions, as with dreams, comes some knowledge of what it is one is seeing. If one is a poet, then the envisioning, the listening, and the writing of the word, are, for that while, fused. For me (and I hope for the reader) this poem *bodies forth* the known material that led to it. Its images could not have been willfully created as mere illustrations of a point. But in mulling over what I knew I felt and thought, I had stirred up levels of imagination, of things I did not know I knew, which made it possible for the poem to emerge in metaphor and find its songlike structure.

There was a lapse of some weeks between these two and the writing of the second "Son" poem. A friend's criticism and my own rereading of "The Disclosure" made it clear to me how insufficient it was, how I had not implied but withheld some of its proper content. I felt the remedy to be a second part, a continuation, rather than a refashioning of what I had already written. I found myself, while I pondered the problem, contemplating a wood-block self-portrait my son had made not long before. What I had before me was not only the print but the actual block of wood with its carved-out surface. Looking at it, I came to realize that "The Disclosure" told only that the boy had begun to wear his heirloom, manhood, and said nothing of his nature. This particular boy-becoming-man moved me for special reasons, after all; reasons which had nothing to do with his being my son, except insofar as that meant I knew something about him. What I was moved by was the capacity for suffering that I had become aware of in him, the suffering for instance of the painful silences of adolescent shyness in a rather conscious and not merely frustrated way; and by the way such experience was beginning to be made over in creative acts. No doubt the writing of "A Man" had intensified this realization for me. This time the first image, which again remained the central image of the poem, although in this case the words changed, was concerned with the woodblock.

> Knives bring forth from the wood
> a man's face, the boy's face in his
> mind's eye, weeping.

This was immediately followed by some lines that were discarded and never reappeared in subsequent drafts:

†I may have had some unconscious recollection of the Days in Emerson's poem of that title.

> *His horseplay,*
> *his loud laughter—their vibrations*
> *still shake some nervous bell*
> *down under, hung in a fern tree—*

The idea here was that his childhood was still so recent that the vibrations of it had only reached Australia, and still had enough force to swing a bell there. I am ignorant in scientific matters and perhaps had misunderstood something I had read about the movement of sound waves and their long life; and my abandonment of this image was a result not only of recognizing its digressiveness—its focusing attention on a side issue—but of my sense that perhaps it was in any case merely fanciful.

The next draft brought in the action of making the wood block:

> *He hacks a slab of wood with*
> *fine knives and there comes into being*
>
> *a grim face, his vision of his own face*
> *down which from one eye*
>
> *rolls a tear—his own face*
> *in the manhood his childhood*
>
> *so swiftly has led to, as a*
> *small brook hastens*
> *into the destiny of a river.*

As you see, I had returned to the river image that had been so persistent in the first poem and yet had been dropped from it in the end. But the rhythms of this draft were wrong. In successive drafts, which I will spare you, as the changes in them are small and confusing, the following revisions were made: "hacks" was excessive and became simply "cuts." "Fine" was omitted as an unnecessary qualification for "knives." The force of "hacks" goes into "violently," and the "fineness" of the knives into "precise," so that "violently precise" says both things together. "Grim" ("a grim face") became first "crisscrossed with lines of longing, of silences endured" and eventually "downstrokes / of silence endured." On the same principle of condensation, synthesis, concretion, "his vision of" becomes "visioned" and "hastens" becomes the more active, particular, visually suggestive "rock-leaping." The more vivid and specific a term is, the more extensive its possibilities of reverberation in the responsive mind. This is the essential meaning of William Carlos Williams's dictum that the universal is found only in the local. However, in one of the discarded drafts it was mentioned that the boy as a child had liked to draw fantastic inventions on graph paper; this was changed to "poster paints," which he had, of course, also used at one time, because in this instance the unique particular seemed likely to be relatively distracting, while poster paints are a widely shared and associative medium that nearly everyone remembers using or has seen their children use. A clause saying that the man's face in the woodblock was "incised as the boy's inward eye / presages" was cut out as redundant.

THE SON

ii The Woodblock

He cuts into a slab of wood,
engrossed, violently precise.
Thus, yesterday, the day before yesterday,
engines of fantasy were evolved
in poster paints. Tonight
a face forms under the knife,

slashed with stern
crisscrosses of longing, downstrokes
of silence endured—
                    his visioned
own face!—
down which from one eye

rolls a tear.
              His own face
drawn from the wood,
deep in the manhood his childhood
so swiftly led to, a small brook rock-leaping
into the rapt, imperious, seagoing river.*

The resolution of the image of the "little river of childhood" into the lines which end the finished poem came, once more, by way of a clearer, deeper *seeing* of the metaphor: once I knew and recorded the way the little river, the brook, leaps over its rocks as it nears a greater stream, I was given the vision of the great river's rapt and majestic presence.

To conclude, I wish to point out that the process I have described does not take place in a condition of alert self-observation. When I looked through my worksheets I *remembered* what I had been doing, what I thought I was after, in each case; but the state of writing, although intense, is dreamy and sensuous, not ratiocinative; and if I had thrown away the worksheets, I would not have been able to reconstruct the history of the poems.

---

*"The Son II," by Denise Levertov, from *The Sorrow Dance.* Copyright © 1965 by Denise Levertov. Reprinted by permission of New Directions.

Memory

Writing is not apart from living. Writing is a kind of double living. The writer experiences everything twice. Once in reality and once more in that mirror which waits always before or behind him.

Catherine Drinker Bowen

David Huddle, originally from the Blue Ridge Mountains of Virginia, now teaches at the University of Vermont and in the Warren Wilson College M.F.A. program in writing. His poetry and fiction have appeared in *Harper's, Esquire, Field, TriQuarterly, Ploughshares,* and the *Hudson Review.* A collection of short stories, *A Dream with No Stump Roots in It* (1975), and his first volume of poetry, *Paper Boy* (1979), both reflect his experiences in the small town where he spent his boyhood, his growth away from family and town, and his more painful experiences in Vietnam. "Memory's Power" was first delivered as a lecture at Goddard College.

Memory's Power

David Huddle

I am sitting in a pick-up truck in Bowling Green, Ohio, with somebody I thought I respected a great deal, and this somebody is telling me that they liked Phil O'Connor's novel, *Stealing Home,* pretty well until they got to know Phil and his kids and their little league experience and all that, and then it didn't seem like the book was all that much of an accomplishment, it was all just the way it was for Phil, he didn't have to make up very much of it at all. I could have argued, but this person had just treated me to ham and eggs and homefries with coffee and the large tomato juice, and I was there in a truck in Bowling Green, where one direction is just about as good as another and it's too flat to argue with anybody, you need altitude, hills and valleys, rocks and crannies, and so on to have a good argument. So I gave this once respected person the kind of look my photographer friend gave me when I told him one day that I thought photography couldn't possibly be an art, all you had to do was take this little, ugly, black machine, and point it somewhere and press a button, that's all there was to it, and what art was there in that?

But now I'm in Vermont, there's plenty of altitude available, and I can argue to my heart's content. Whether or not it's all right to write real stuff and call it fiction is the question. I do realize that there *is* an argument here: there are two sides to be put forth, and the other side often seems very attractive to me. I certainly believed Ay Kwai Armah when he said, in a workshop at

Source: *By permission of David Huddle.*

Columbia, after a reading of a particularly charged piece of autobiographical fiction, that that kind of writing, was, for the author, like spending capital instead of spending interest: you'd run out of it soon, if you kept doing it.

John Irving seems to me persuasive when he says—and here I'm paraphrasing remarks I've heard him make in lectures, workshops, and conversations at Bread Loaf—that "because something actually happened is no reason whatsoever for including it in a fiction," when he says that purely autobiographical novelists usually have only one good book in them, and when he says that autobiographical writing often indicates a failure of the imagination.

And John Cheever could say just about anything he wanted to, and I'd be nodding my head, yes, yes. Here Cheever is, in an interview in the *New York Times,* putting autobiography in its place:

> It seems to me that any confusion between autobiography and fiction debases fiction. The role autobiography plays in fiction is precisely the role that reality plays in a dream. As you dream your ship, you perhaps know the boat, but you're going towards a coast that is quite strange; you're wearing strange clothes, the language that is being spoken around you is a language you don't understand, but the woman on your left is your wife. It seems to me that this not capricious but quite mysterious union of fact and imagination one also finds in fiction. My favorite definition of fiction is Cocteau's: "Literature is a force of memory that we have not yet understood." It seems that in a book one finds gratifying, the writer is able to present the reader with a memory he has already possessed, but has not comprehended. . . .

And that seems right to me, it makes me want to nod my head when I read it, even though it's contrary to what I want to put forth here. A lot of good people have a lot of bad things to say about the use of autobiography in fiction, and they seem to lift their voices when they speak on this particular subject, as if they really feel strongly about it: *keep autobiography out of fiction.*

But my recent experience has been to write a book of autobiographical poems (which is o.k.; the poets don't get as fired up on the subject as the fiction writers do) and a sequence of six long autobiographical stories. I didn't start out writing that way. I began with made-up stories, probably for the same reason that most everybody else does; I took the word *fiction* literally and wrote imagined stories, stories with made-up characters and made-up events.

I feel a little bit guilty nowadays about writing so autobiographically. So much so, in fact, that I put a disclaimer in my book of poems that says, "These poems are fictions. The truth they attempt to achieve is personal and imaginative, not historical." What that amounts to is telling a lie that these true poems are lies. Well, some of them are. It gets complicated. I put that disclaimer in partly because I felt bad at having used—and that's the word that applies here, *used*—so much of what actually happened in my family and in the town where I grew up. But I also put it in because my wife's a lawyer, and she assured me that some of the people in my poems, Pig Clemons, Jeep Alley, Deetum Dunford, Monkey, Dude, Hat, and Hitler Dunford, Phoenix Hill, Geronimo Spraker, and so on, might like to sue their old buddy David Huddle, haul him into a court of law. I can't quite feature being sued for something I put into a poem, but the idea makes me nervous. So I put my disclaimer in, and now I'm safe, if just a little guilty-feeling.

I'm also grateful, to autobiography, because I was given those poems and stories to write at a time when I had just about given up on myself as a story-writer. My made-up stories had become shorter, thinner, more fragile. I knew the next one I wrote was going to disappear right in front of me, it was going to unwrite itself as I took each page out of the typewriter. When I speak of autobiographical fiction here, I mean stories whose basic impulse comes out of memory. If the thing begins in memory, no matter how much made-up stuff it has in it, I consider the story to be autobiographical.

The stories my students gave me in my first years of teaching were successful for various reasons, maybe a different reason for every story, and those reasons seemed to me only vaguely connected to anything I said or did in class, anything I allegedly taught. But when the stories were unsuccessful, they were unsuccessful for a few reasons that I could clearly and positively name:

—The unsuccessful stories were too abstract and not concrete enough. They were too much of the mind and not enough of the senses. About this, Wei T'ai, an eleventh century Chinese poet says, "Poetry presents the thing in order to convey the feeling. It should be precise about the thing and reticent about the feeling, for as soon as the mind responds and connects with the thing, the feeling shows in the words; this is how poetry enters deeply into us." Allen Tate, in *The Fathers,* says, "There is not an old man living who can recover the emotions of the past; he can only bring back the objects around which, secretly, the emotions have ordered themselves in memory." And Flannery O'Connor, to whom I am more than willing to give the last word, says, "The beginning of human knowledge is through the senses, and the fiction writer begins where human perception begins." This abstract/concrete business is the main issue I deal with in my writing classes. At the end of every semester I am sick of hearing myself say the same thing about it that I said in the first classes. Like most of the crucial issues of story writing, it's a point that's so true and obvious there's no shock value in it.

—The unsuccessful stories were inadequately considered. Which is to say that the writer didn't work as hard as his story wanted him to. The writer did not hold the material in his mind and heart for an adequate amount of time. He did not bring all of his mental and emotional strength to the story. He did not revise enough. I am always telling my stories that I can finish them in three or four drafts, and they are always telling me that I can't finish them in fewer than seven or eight drafts. I have more than once told myself that if I had known how much work writing stories was going to be, I would never gotten involved with it. Right this minute I have several unsuccessful stories of my own on my desk at home, and these mock me each time I look at them. "You did not give us enough," they say. "When will you come to us and give us everything?"

—Finally, the unsuccessful stories I received from my students were written by a false self. In most cases this false self is an overly literary fellow, a user of fancy diction and elaborate syntax, a manipulator of characters who are too good and beautiful for this world or else who are so thoroughly terrible and evil that a reader might keep his children indoors for days if he took them seriously, and these characters usually sit still, making grand speeches to each other or thinking profound thoughts to themselves until the right moment, when violence is called for. Thomas Williams writes about a writer of such stories in his novel, *The Hair of Harold Roux;* Harold Roux, who wears a wig, ignores his own history, of growing up in a coal town, in order to write about a pretty life he wishes he'd had among the rich and beautiful.

The reasons for writing out of a false self are various and complicated. Wish fulfillment may have a lot to do with it. Maybe we ought to be forgiven for writing wishfully, for presenting ourselves as much more heroic, intelligent, right-thinking, effectual, articulate, ecological, potent, and good-smelling than we actually are. But it is the way of the good readers, the ones we really want, not to be forgiving of wish-fulfillment.

I have been reluctant to assign subjects to my students: write about a chase, a trip, a baby, an older person, somebody looking out a window, an argument, that sort of thing. It has seemed to me that choosing a subject is one of the few democratic aspects of an activity that I consider so demanding as to be almost totalitarian in character. But in pondering these three reasons—and some others—for many of my students' turning out unsuccessful stories, I hit upon the notion of restricting them to autobiographical material as a way of directing them to potentially better stories. For a summer school course, I made up a questionnaire that forced students to explore just about all the memory they had available to them. You'd be surprised how many of us feel that our own lives are not literarily worthy, our own lives are just not interesting enough, we'd have to write about somebody else. My questionnaire demonstrated to all of us that we did have material to write about, we didn't have to be so humble about our dumb, boring lives. Writers who try exploring their own histories are often surprised at what happens. A good many people would say, "I can't remember all those things. It's too far back."

You do not, even those of you with very strong memories, remember whole chunks of your lives. You remember in small pieces, fragments, maybe just the way the light of a summer morning shown through the curtains of your bedroom when you first woke up one day thirty or forty years ago. But when you sit down to write, you discover that *one thing leads to another,* and that in the act of writing, you can recover many fragments of your life that have been lost to you; you can begin to recover whole chunks of your history. "It's all back there somewhere," one of my informed friends told me, tapping the back of his head. If you think about that bedroom curtain, you remember, of course, that it was green, that it had a musty smell about it if you put your nose near it, that your mother made it, that she made matching bedspreads for you and your brother, and that you would stand beside the sewing machine and talk with her sometimes while she worked, and you had to be quiet when she was peddling, and, and, and. . . .

Memory and imagination are our only resources. Our stories are either remembered or imagined or—and this is most often the case—they are both remembered and imagined, they come out of a combining of the two resources. In both memory and imagination, one thing leads to another. I tell my classes that the most important decisions and discoveries in my own writing have occurred between one sentence and the next, between one paragraph and the next. During the two little thwacks my thumb makes on the space bar after I've thunked down a period with the fourth finger of my right hand—during that little piece of space and time, I hope to receive, if only occasionally, the whole force of what we call "creativity," which may in fact be just the process of one thing leading to another, the energy of the imagination, the energy of memory. And that's probably the strongest argument I know for sitting down to the paper and getting on with it rather than going into the other room to pace and think and wait.

Stories that work soothe me. I remember them by way of details, scenes, sentences, dialogues. I remember them, I cherish them, I savor them over the years. I still grin to myself over the story that Judy Towne, a sophomore from Milton, Vermont, wrote for a class of mine several years ago, a story in which a girl and a boy meet at a party, leave and go down the hall to a dormitory room where they talk about cooking pizza, and in that conversation it becomes clear to them that romance is not possible for them. When stories don't work, I forget them, everything in them, all the details. That's the ultimate form of literary revenge; it's what you do to a bad story instead of shooting it.

The story that doesn't work because it's overly abstract is usually the result of the beginning writer's misconception, his belief that his task is primarily intellectual and that he must be profound. Flannery O'Connor addresses the point forcefully when she says that "there's a certain grain of stupidity that the writer of fiction can hardly do without, and this is the quality of having to stare, of not getting the point at once." And Robertson Davies says that "All sorts of people expect writers to be intellectuals. Sometimes they are, but it is not necessary to their work. . . . I do not say that writers are childlike creatures of untutored genius; often they are intelligent people, but the best part of their intelligence is of the feeling and intuitive order."

I could tell my students in the beginning that you don't have to be smart to write well, which is certainly in large part true, but I expect they'd resist the notion. They're sitting there in that classroom in the first place because, as they've probably been told many times, they have good minds. Most of us have been taught that it is a lot better to be smart than to be stupid. We are taught to respect intellect, and I suspect that we are also taught to disrespect the senses. Usually when we think of how our senses come into use, we think of dope, loud music, drunkenness, eating too much.

So there is a kind of reversal of values that must take place for a writer to begin to write good, concrete stories. He must learn to respect the senses—Joseph Conrad advised us that "All art... appeals primarily to the senses, and the artistic aim when expressing itself in written words must also make its appeal through the senses.... " I believe that the beginning writer must learn at least some disrespect for the intellect, just enough disrespect to keep his mind from spoiling his material.

We may have been taught to intellectualize almost everything around us, but we remember our own lives in almost purely sensuous terms. In my classroom, I may get up on my academic high horse and begin to discourse on the fragmented existential universe suggested through exotic diction, erratic syntax, pessimistic humor, and cunningly random structure in the fictions of Donald Barthelme, but when I write, out of memory, of a summer morning of my early childhood, it goes like this:

> *Just at the foot of her front porch were her pink tea roses. My grandmother, in her white dress, her white stockings, the prim little black lace-up shoes, stood with her hand behind one of the small opening rosebuds. "Isn't this lovely?" she asked. She put her nose near the pink flower. It was the middle of a hot day. Her grey hair shone in the sunlight. The roses smelled sweet and hot, as if they were cooking.*

My point here is simply that autobiographical writing leads us naturally toward concrete writing, toward language that involves the nose, tongue, ears, skin, and especially the eyes, as well as the mind.

A misconception is also responsible for the inadequately considered story. The notion here is that writers are clever devils, skillful manipulators of their audiences, primarily technicians. Out of this misconception come stories that may be mildly interesting but that are simply *not felt*, stories that lack conviction. Hayden Carruth, in *Harper's*, speaks exactly to this point when he says, "Let there be passion, along with talent.... Passionate vision, passionate concern: these make works of art." And John Irving, in *The Washington Post Book World*, is also speaking to the point when he says,

> *I had a class of graduate-student writers, once. Their favorite story—written by one of them—was a story about a three-course meal from the point of view of a fork. The fork was the main character. It was a very sophisticated piece of writing, and brilliantly funny. In the end, in an especially well-written scene, the fork got thrown out in the trash. The only problem was: I wasn't sad about what happened to the fork. The entire experience of the story was intellectual. It was the best story I ever read about a poor fork—but I am not a fork, and I don't care what a fork feels.*

For the writer who sees his job as primarily technical, one thing is as good as another; a fork as subject matter is just as valid as the French Revolution, an asparagus patch just as powerful as an Ahab, a Sutpen, or a Gatsby. In fact it is this arbitrariness that is a primary virtue of "the new fiction." Donald Barthelme, a writer who's done some wonderful stories but whose work all too often lets me put it down before I've finished it, begins one of his *New Yorker* stories this way:

> *When Captain Blood goes to sea, he locks the doors and windows of his house on Cow Island, personally. When Captain Blood, at sea, paces the deck, he usually paces the foredeck rather than the afterdeck—a matter of personal prefer-ence. He keeps marmalade and a spider monkey in his cabin, and four perukes on stands.*

I see virtues of language and wit in such a paragraph, but when I have tried it out, I don't feel compelled to go on to the next paragraph. I feel that the objects in this paragraph—the afterdeck and the foredeck, the marmalade, the spider monkey, and the four perukes on stands—are like stuff the writer has thrown out of the back of a closet. If one thing is as good as any other thing, then nothing makes much difference, whatever the closet offers is good enough.

What I want in a story, and I suspect it is what most people want, is the quality of passion and of *necessity*. I don't want what the writer tosses out of his closet onto the floor behind him; I want his best brandy, and I want him to take me to the special room where he keeps the thing in the house that he cares about most, and I want him to tell me about it in such a way that I begin to care for that thing, too.

There are fine writers who achieve stories of passion and necessity wholly through the imagination. Kafka's "The Metamorphosis" is the shining example, and here are its first two sentences:

> *As Gregor Samsa awoke one morning from uneasy dreams he found himself transformed in his bed into a gigantic insect. He was lying on his hard, as if it were armor-plated, back and when he lifted his head a little he could see his dome-like brown belly divided into stiff arched segments on top of which the bed quilt could hardly keep in position and was about to slide off completely.*

The first sentence might have given me some doubts about whether or not to go on, but the second, with its rigorous working out of the consequences of the first—if the man has turned into an insect and just awakened, then this must be what his first perceptions would be—is so urgently necessary that I feel that I must go on to the third, and so on.

But Kafka is exceptional. Most writers are, in my opinion, most passionate when they are working out of memory, or mostly out of memory. We will take liberties with made-up characters, made-up lives, but we become more responsible when we are dealing with our own life and the lives of those people who are important to us. Complexity may have something to do with it. We know our own experience to have been enormously complicated, and if we are to write about it, we feel that we must catch something of the nature of that complication. We resist simplification. We resist the arbitrary. In our own lives, we know that things happened in a certain way, and those things were necessarily *that way* and not some other way. When we are using the material of our own history, we are most likely to find passion and to engage in that rigorous weighing and balancing of chance and choice, of surprise and inevitability, that the well-considered story requires of us. I believe that memory is the most likely route for a writer to follow in locating material about which he can write passionately and urgently. Working through memory, we are most likely to avoid the arbitrary and to make connections in our stories that are necessary, inevitable, and meaningful. We may very well want to be surprised by a story as we are reading it. But when we have come to the end, and we are looking back at it, reflecting, we want to have a sense that what happened in that story was inevitable, want to be able to say, yes, that's how it would have gone.

Memory operates by way of the senses, by way of detail, which is the stuff of fiction, the fabric of good stories. For me, memory serves as real stuff, material, matter, fabric, clay, bricks and mortar, lumber and nails, plaster, what have you. The use of memory makes the act of writing more craftsman-like, if you will. Humbler. Tom Wolfe (speaking at the University of Michigan) says that "when you're in your late teens or early twenties and you want to write, you want to feel that the only thing that matters is your genius. The material, the content of the writer's work, is merely the clay, the wax, that Himself is going to use." I can remember feeling that way, but I can also remember feeling nervous about it, anxious, knowing even then, as I think everyone knows at any age, that talent is fragile, talent is luck, talent is given and so talent might be taken away at any time. Nowadays I know I am not the graceful magician who makes a story come into being, poof, out of thin air. I do hope to be the slow worker who drives the truck with a busted muffler and a back end that's got in it every kind of brick, pipe, board, wire, string, tool, and scrap, and piece of something that I ever might need.

What can be said *against* trying to write autobiographical fiction? John Irving names two negative aspects with his phrase, "the tyranny and self-importance of autobiography in fiction."

By tyranny I understand him to mean the power that personal fact brings to bear on the writer. If we know that an event happened in a certain way, it is very difficult for us to change it, even though the aesthetic requirements of our story might demand change. There is a kind of rigidness, or more accurately maybe, *brittleness,* about autobiographical material that might be described as tyranny. The writer who would use the material to make stories must be able to let go of what he knows to be historical truth, must be willing to lie and to revise that historical truth into imaginative truth.

By self-importance I understand John Irving to mean the writer who uses his writing to promote himself. It is true that autobiographical fiction writing can bring out the worst in anybody, the would-be celebrity who has just been waiting for a chance to tell the world about himself, the preacher-educator who wants to correct the deviant behavior of everyone else through the revelation of his own exemplary life, and so on. We are all of us, writers and non-writers, to ourselves heroes, unrecognized heroes, of the stories we imagine ourselves to be living; everything we do or say is an effort to make the rest of the world conspire in our personal fictions, our personal protagonism. If we practice autobiography without rigorous self-judgment, which is the balancing opposite of self-importance, the result probably will be obnoxious.

Writing autobiographically involves not only revealing ourselves to the world—which although frightening is also a little bit thrilling—but also writing about others, our family-members, our friends, our enemies. Diplomatic relations can be strained. There can be a lot of trouble. I remember Peter Taylor's sheepish look when he told of his father meeting him at the airport once to tell Peter that if he'd been around when the father read that story that Peter'd published somewhere about Aunt So-And-So, the father would have punched him in the face. I have a sickening memory of a telephone conversation I had with my parents just after they'd read a story of mine, about Vietnam, which was published in *Esquire* while my younger brother was stationed at Cam Ranh Bay. My own personal record is not exemplary, but in spite of my record, my obvious hypocrisy notwithstanding, I think I have good advice to offer: I believe the writer must do whatever he can to avoid such trouble, to keep from hurting feelings, but I believe finally he cannot allow the opinions and feelings of others to stop or to interfere with his writing. Maybe this is the ultimate selfishness, to say that one's own work is more important than the feelings of family and friends. Autobiographical writing will bring you to the point of having to make not just one but a number of hard choices between the life and the work.

Almost every semester in the classroom, I am asked the very good question: for whom do we write. I try to answer up as loudly as I can and with no more than an instant's hesitation, "We write for ourselves first, and then we write for others." The question isn't an easy one, and my answer is more like a mantra for me—a formula I might say to myself over and over to give myself comfort. In story-writing there is always that torturous measuring of self and other: on the one hand I might be writing this story about this insensitive sister and her nincompoop husband, writing it with total disregard for what my real sister and brother-in-law think about me. And maybe that's admirable—if it's a good story, it's a lot more admirable than if it's a bad one. But I might also be writing the story so that my younger brother, the one my real sister was always tattling on, will love me better. And can I really ever say, I wrote this story for me and for no one else? Or for my younger brother, or the reader at the edge of the forest, for the fisherman out at dawn, for anybody anywhere, real or imagined? The more you worry that question, the more you have to back away from it to keep from falling into it and disappearing. But I think there is a better answer than the one I've been offering. For whom do we write? *We write for the work itself.* We ourselves are devious, complicated, finally unknowable even to ourselves, and you others out there are devious and complicated and certainly unknowable to me. Experience washes over us and is gone forever. The world rushes at us and then rushes away from us, and as Country Joe and the Fish put it so succinctly, "Whoopee, we're all gonna die." *We write for the work itself.* Because the work stays. Because the work may very well be devious and complicated, but it is a rock, it will hold steady, it will be regarded, it is finally knowable.

In the first place we write for the work itself. In the second place we write for ourselves. And in the third place we write for others. This civilized ordering (work, self, others) does not ignore the reader, nor does it intrude upon the writer's own integrity. It simply puts first things first: whether writing from memory or from imagination, whether using fantasy or autobiography—in this ecstasy of my conclusion the materials have come not to matter so much any more—the first consideration is this, to make the thing beautiful. No matter who sees it.

Glenn F. Jackson worked as editor and reporter for several small town newspapers before he received his M.F.A. from the State University of Iowa Writers' Workshop. His poems and stories have appeared in more than thirty national literary magazines and journals, including *The Virginia Quarterly Review*, the *Michigan Quarterly*, and the *Mississippi Review*. "The beginning of writing," he observes, "is letting out the voice inside you—of finding that voice and listening to it until you can hear the rhythm of its language." Several journals have recognized his work with honors including The Most Distinctive American Short Story (1966) and the Best Literary Magazine Fiction (1967). Jackson is currently working on a collection of short stories based on memories of a small Missouri town.

Glenn F. Jackson

That was the summer I moved closer to pain and death than I wanted to, that summer of my gimpy knee. It was Mother's Day, 1943, and my mother and sister and I had gone to spend the day with my Uncle Hubert's family. I was seven and my sister was five. My cousin, Erman, was also five.

It was early evening and the three of us were playing in the yard. We had just about exhausted our repertoire of games and decided to play a new kind of tag. The "IT" player, or chaser, would have to put something over his head so he couldn't see the others in the game. We found a small cardboard box that fit over our heads easily and began the game.

It was fun to watch the chaser running around blindly, tripping and stumbling, and sometimes falling, as we tried to get closer and closer without getting caught. Finally, however, I was too bold and was tagged. I confidently placed the box over my own head and started running. We were in the yard which was large and grassy and free from trees. There was only one obstacle, near the back fence: a large rubbish heap of wood ashes and garbage.

I was running wild and free, chasing the happy, laughing voices of my sister and my cousin. I lost my balance and started to fall. I heard my sister scream, and then I cried out in pain. My left knee was on fire, and I clawed at the box on my head. When the box was off, I looked at the place where my knee was supposed to be and it seemed far away. My knee burned and I could feel the blood

Source: *By permission of Glenn F. Jackson.*

sliding down and filling my shoe. I moaned but didn't cry. I looked at the rubbish pile. The jagged edge of a piece of rusty stovepipe was sticking out of the ashes.

By then my Uncle Hubert and Aunt Lucy and my mother had rushed out of the house. This was 1943, in a small town in Missouri; there was a war going on and there were very few cars in that town. I listened as the grownups tried to decide what to do. Despite the pain, I felt only like an interested bystander.

Then Uncle Hubert picked me up again and started down the road to a neighbor's house. I heard someone say the man knew First-Aid. By that time the man and his wife were outside. The man ripped away my trouser leg and poured kerosene on my knee. As the kerosene washed the blood away, I saw that my knee was almost cut in two. The gaping flesh showed the white bones inside where my kneecap was supposed to be. I wondered what was keeping my leg from falling off. From the gasps and cries of the others I guessed they were wondering the same thing.

The man, who I later came to know as Archie Smith, tore a bed sheet into strips and bandaged my leg. Archie Smith had a car and Uncle Hubert carried me to it and put me on the back seat. My mother got in beside me. The road to Salem then was gravel, and everytime we hit a bump or chug hole my leg throbbed. Thirty miles and what seemed like thirty hours later we got to the doctor's office. A long time later that night my leg and knee was clamped together and bandaged loosely in gauze. I didn't feel any pain.

The next morning the pain was almost unbearable. We went back to the doctor's. I knew something was wrong, but no one would tell me what it was. Years later my mother would tell me that the excruciating pain was caused by blood poisoning, and the doctor feared gangrene. He wanted to amputate: my leg for my life. My mother had to decide; my father was in the war. She said she preferred death to a one-legged son. We returned home, and for a week my mother never left my bedside. When the pain caused me to cry out, she would soak my knee with alcohol and massage my leg until the pain subsided. In the end her perseverance overcame the infection.

As it was, I did not walk again for nearly three months.

This is the way I remember the actual experience from my own life which led to the prose version you have just read, and how I originally recorded it in my journal. Later, as I reread this account, the experience pulled me inside it so that I began to relive it in my imagination. But reliving the incident, which produced the following poem, led to a new experience.

THE WALKING WOUNDED

*This is the summer
of my gimpy knee, 1943,
that war far away—the other one—
and the day a holiday for mothers.*

In the yard the grass stood
proudly at attention,
to honor flowers
that walked in beauty.
At Uncle Hubert's we dinnered
on rationed meat
before invading that yard.
Three laughing children
who played tag and hide-and-seek
were not the only invaders
that festive, carefree day.
At the rear,
while an enemy bayonet waited,
I was the one who strayed.
My knee severed
to the bone, that wound
too deep for bleeding.
In three months
I was back among
the walking wounded,
the only casualty
in our little town.
We survive or do not survive
these continuing wounds.
The world wins some.

As you can see, there are significant differences between the prose account and the poem about my injured knee. One of these differences is the selection of details. The prose version reports everything that actually happened, or as much as I can remember. The poem leaves out most of this. However, using prose entries from my journal is one of the ways I have of getting into the writing process so that it is frequently successful for me. And it is the writing process, which I think of as a journey, that I am going to talk about. But first some introductory comments.

The reason for the success of my own process, I feel, is that using a prose version of an experience gives me a ready source of images to work from. As I read what I've written in my journal, these images on the page start to flow through my imagination. And then as I recreate these images something exciting happens; they feed back into my imagination and cause new and more deeply felt images to surface and join, or, as it frequently happens, to replace the existing conscious images. When I start to see and feel these priming images clearly and vividly, they usually free my imagination so that entirely new images flow readily.

When this happens, I must be willing to follow the new images wherever they want to take me. I have to be ready and willing to let them lead me away from the actual experience. I have found that if I'm willing to trust myself, or my imagination, as William Stafford has said, something is always there. And if I follow these new images, the something that is there which they lead me to is almost always more intense and original than the literal experience. Which brings me to what I've been trying to say all along: that for me the writing process is a journey of exploration and discovery of experience but which is made through my imagination.

In the journal account of my injured knee, I had to stay on the subject because I was finding out about the experience and what I could say about it as I reported it. But in the poem, produced from my imagination, I was already familiar with the actual experience and knowing this freed my imagination to explore around inside it to see if it would lead me someplace different. As a result of this freedom, the exploration led me to a deeper part of the imagination into a blood-remembering. I was no longer merely reporting a personal experience but some primitive or primary knolwedge of the human imagination; of the blood. In other words, by probing deeply and freely enough, I went back to one of our lost and forgotten human beginnings.

But I see now, as I try to reconstruct what was happening during the making of this poem, that I was aware not only of images but also some aspect or structure of the language. I don't remember being consciously aware of the language, but I must have had some level of awareness, for I discovered in looking over my first draft that while I was concentrating on seeing the images clearly at the beginning I jotted a line in the margin of the page. When I saw and felt the image of the walking wounded, which I expressed in the lines: "In three months/I was back among/the walking wounded," I then wrote without pausing or consulting the words I had written in the margin the concluding lines: "the only casualty/in our little town."

The words I had written in the margin were: "the only casualty/in our little town." I don't know what to make of this, but I mention it because I was in a trance while the poem was being made. In this trance-like condition, I see both images and words clearly. When an image demands to be heard, it flashes onto the screen in my mind both visually and verbally. What this suggests is that the language part of the brain functions at a sub-conscious level as well as the visual brain when the imagination is fully engaged. This is conjecture. All I know is that when I write, if the images are present, clearly and vividly, and intensely felt, the language to express them is also present.

Many people are uncomfortable with the term "automatic writing." Nearly all of my writing is automatic, that is, it happens if I let it. Or maybe it would be better to say, when I can't prevent it. I often feel when I'm writing that I'm merely an instrument. I think that "merely" is the word that bothers a lot of people. Perhaps I shouldn't say merely. A lot of people might feel better if I said that I feel like a human instrument. Yes, that's better, because that's the way I feel about my writing.

I am the instrument through which some of our lost human beginnings surface and are found again. I don't mean to sound grandiose, and I don't want to give you the impression that I'm trying to romanticize the noble savage. I'm only trying to say that civilization, instead of mastering the beast in us, has merely turned us into another kind of beast. If we could discover and learn our lost beginnings, we might have a better chance of becoming human. We might make peace with the world and with ourselves.

But this is supposed to be a discussion of the writing process, which I have identified as a journey of exploration and discovery. For me it is a long journey, a lifetime journey undertaken to explore familiar but unknown territory. The territory is familiar because it is my own individual experience. It is unknown because I am not exploring the actual experience but instead I am moving around inside the experience to find out what the imagination has turned it into.

Of the two activities—exploration and discovery—exploration is more important. The reason seems clear. We often are not aware of discoveries when we make them and even when we are aware of having made a discovery many times we are unable to talk about it. At least, not in rational language. That's why we write the poem: to express the images of our discoveries.

Images are the language of the imagination; words are the language of our rational mind. The imagination is primary; the rational mind is secondary. It is through the rational or secondary language that we reach agreement with one another about the meaning and importance of our common, shared experiences. It is the imagination that makes it possible for each of us to reach agreement with ourselves. The imagination makes it possible for us to possess our own experiences, to regain our genuine selves.

Few of us have total recall, but even if we possessed a photographic memory, it wouldn't help us much since memory serves our secondary mind. It only helps us to see how our experiences are like everyone else's. The imagination is where we go to discover what is unique and individual about these common human experiences.

The imagination is the memory of the race, the human animal. It is here that we have to go if we want to learn what our distant ancestors knew, to explore and discover those natural human instincts and impulses that have been civilized out of us. It is the imagination that makes it possible for us to explore our blood memories, those memories that make our spiritual as well as our physical survival possible.

When we explore our imagination, we return to the ancient places of our lost beginnings. These, however, are not simply geographical locations; by place, I mean states of imagination, sources of awareness, the awareness of our own relationship to the natural world, our connections with all other life.

There is a strong sense of place in my writing, place meaning, as I've said, both geography and imaginative consciousness. For the reader who is not familiar with my background, the place of imaginative consciousness may seem more obvious. But without my own awareness of the actual geographical place, I probably couldn't have made the poem I have been talking about in these pages.

Readers of my poems and stories have often expressed surprise at my seemingly precocious awareness of place. Frequently, they have asked me, "How could you have been aware of that so young?" For a long time, I couldn't answer their question. I usually stammered something like, "Well, I experienced this when I was seven, or nine," or some other tender age. I know now how close my answer was to the truth of the matter.

I have always had a strong sense of place. At first, I was aware only of the geography and not the imaginative sensibility. When people asked me what I wrote about, I usually told them: "Young boys and old men." The answer seemed reasonably accurate since a lot of my writing has been focused on these subjects.

I hope the following statement doesn't seem too neat and convenient, but in my imagination I am always the young boy trying to discover what old men know. My imagination is as ancient as the first human who sensed his relationship to the natural world, who knew how his life was connected to all living things. But it is youthfulness of my imagination which frees me from the secondary rational process so that I can return to the beginning when humans were still filled with the awesome beauty and terror of their mortal existence.

When my creative process is working, I feel these ancient voices calling to me. I have said my mind is in a trance; I feel mesmerized, totally oblivious to the immediate world around me. I experience visions of familiar people and places. I can see and touch and hear them. I feel that if I can trust them they will tell me what they mean.

By getting in touch with these visions, I am able to create my own human myths, the myths I live by. These are probably common to the human species, but I have to imagine and live them for myself if they are to mean anything. By exploring and discovering them through the creative process, I become aware of what it is in my own human experience that gives them their uniqueness and reality.

In other words, what I'm suggesting is that each of us is his own maker of myths. The archetypal myths have been bastardized so that they don't mean anything to most humans. They are vague and distant, or distant and frightening. They become real again and somehow less frightening when we can create them for ourselves.

The idea of writing as a journey takes on greater significance if my perception of the process is valid. As I've said, all I have to do is make the journey. I am not concerned about writing literature. I am not bound by social and literary interpretations of the archetypal myths because I am creating my own.

The written product, that is, the poem or story, matters only insofar as it lets or helps you see where you've been so you can go on. But it is a hindrance if it makes it impossible for you to move on, to try to get someplace else. You cannot depend on the product to show you where you should go next or how to get there, and you'll be disappointed if you think it ought to. Each poem or story is a singular part of the journey, but all it can do is make it possible for you to start on other journeys.

Or better yet, you should think of the written product as part of a continuing journey. Each product is simply a piece of the long journey we have broken off usually for convenience's sake. In other words, each product is simply a part of the one poetical journey we are continually making and writing. But because we have to stop from time to time, we arbitrarily break off or separate parts of the journey and label them as products.

It might be more helpful for us to think of the products or pieces as rest stops along the way. This could lessen the emphasis we give to the separate products. We would be better off concentrating our efforts on making the journey.

If we did this, no single part would be more significant than any other. If we looked at our writing in this way, we might break down some of the self-imposed barriers we put in our way. By looking at our poems as products, we are constantly comparing their value and success. Each time we sit down to write we tell ourselves that we have to do better, that we have to improve on what we've done before.

If we thought of the writing process as a journey, we wouldn't have to be continually making these comparisons. Our only constraints would be finding or making the time we need to continue the journey. But when we concentrate on individual poems as finished products, it's as though we're saying to ourselves: "I came this far today. This is where I've gotten on this attempt. Tomorrow I still have to get over to there, to that place. And I've got to get there in better shape than I did today. I've got to go a lot farther tomorrow. And tomorrow. . . . "

But if we think of the poems only as rest stops, we can say, or we only need to say: "This is today's journey. Tomorrow I'll continue on my way, and I'll trust myself to go on." If we could learn to think this way, no single part of the journey would take on more importance than any other part of it. Making the journey would be what is important.

If we stopped being so critical, we might find ourselves freer to try different ways of making the journey. I don't mean we would consciously make radical departures from traditional forms and procedures. We would not consciously do anything. That's the point.

My ability to make the journey, to create my own myths comes from my awareness of place as geography. Even in my consciousness, but particularly in my imagination, I am never far away from my place. I know the land intimately where I grew up. I believe I could draw you a map of my place that would take you to any place you want to go within a fifty-mile radius.

This little piece of land is the source of my imagination. When I go home I walk the same fields and woods I walked as a boy. And as my imagination fills up my blood begins to remember. I go back through generation after generation. From myself as man to boy, from my father to my grandfather; from my grandfather to my great-grandfather. I go back farther and farther until I am one of the first aborigines walking that land.

And now the rational mind produces a paradox. I must return to those distant places and there lose my conscious self in order to find my real self. It is there that I find what really does exist, not just what seems to exist. It is there that I see and touch my tribal gods and the natural gods and learn what the conditions for living are.

When I know these things in my blood, when I feel them, I know they will talk to me in my writing. I go away then and write them when they come to me.

Sometimes I feel they have temporarily deserted me. Or I do something that keeps them from coming to me. Whenever this happens, I find a way to go home again. This frees me, for they are always there. I continue the journey. It promises to go on and on.

Wright Morris is one of America's most respected and enduring novelists whose work seems to grow stronger in his later stages. With over thirty books of fiction and essays, he remains best known for those that focus on Nebraska, his home state, and especially for the novel, *Ceremony in Lone Tree* (1960), "The Ram in the Thicket," a now classic short story, and *The Territory Ahead* (1958), essays on American literature. Morris has received three Guggenheim Fellowships and the National Book Award for *The Field of Vision* (1956). Although he taught at San Francisco State College for thirteen years, he has spent most of his life as a professional writer. In recent years he has made his home in Mill Valley, California, where he and his wife have produced a number of photo texts. His most recent novel, *Plains Songs: For Female Voices* (1980), received wide critical acclaim, as did *Will's Boy* (1981), the autobiography of his childhood.

Origins

Reflections on
Emotion, Memory, and Imagination

Wright Morris

In my second novel, *The Man Who Was There,* published in 1945, a character ponders the ceaseless accumulation of lint and dust under the bed. Where, she wonders, does it all come from? After almost forty years of fiction writing I am led to ask the same question. Is it substantially imagination, or memory? It is well known that fiction writers have long memories, and draw on them often. So do most people, or the writer's memory would be of little interest. In the main he reminds us of what we remember about ourselves. In much of modern fiction we seem to see more of memory than imagination. Writers remember what happened, then embellish on it, even if it happened only last week. I still have a vivid memory of the occasion my own memory was singled out for admiration. "What a memory you have!" the reader told me, who happened to be from my home state of Nebraska. He could testify that what I remembered was part of the truth, if not all of it. "I was right there," he said, "but I'd forgotten most of it. Reading your book brought it all back." I thanked him. It was not a small thing to bring it all back, whatever it was.

I have been more attentive to memory, since my debt was pointed out. Was that what I was doing? Remembering what others had forgotten? That reader had particular praise for what I remembered about Lone Tree, the site

Source: *Reprinted from* Conversations with Wright Morris *edited by Robert E. Knoll, by permission of the University of Nebraska Press. Copyright © 1977 by the University of Nebraska Press.*

of *Ceremony in Lone Tree.* I had been too pleased (and tactful) to suggest that Lone Tree had no existence in fact but was the fabrication of a writer who showed little or no total recall. Lone Tree was to be found only in the novel, not on the map. Regrettably, this admission disenchants many readers and leads them to question the writer's sources. How is one to know he knows what he is doing? This reader particularly liked a chapter in the novel called *The Scene,* seeded with the objects and the details in which I seem to take so much interest. There was that fly at the window, the one trapped between the cracked blind and the pane. How well the reader remembered that identical fly! He also recalled how, as a boy, he had buried the white hairs pulled from a mare's tail in a barrel of rainwater, but it had skipped his mind what had then happened, if anything. For filling him in on all of that, he was grateful. This reader could appreciate, as many could not, who had not been born and raised in the Platte Valley, the pleasure of tagging along, barefoot, in the wake of the watersprinkler. He felt sure he had seen that particular sprinkler on his last trip back.

His comment reminded me that my own bare feet had gone unsprinkled. A real loss or a slip of memory? In another town, led on by a scoundrel, I repeatedly looted an ice wagon. In the ice we sucked, strange things were frozen. What they were I was free to imagine. Is it in such a manner that the fiction writer redeems lost time?

I see now that much of my plains-based fiction grew out of my need for an experience I came too late for. The signal example is the town of Lone Tree itself, first observed, in passing, in *The World in the Attic,* a suitable realm and dwelling place for the likes of Tom Scanlon. Once that fact was determined, the appropriate details assembled about his person. They settled into their places, their roles, as icons: a hotel, a lone tree, a railroad, a cattle loader. These artifacts constituted "the scene" in the way movable props located a Western movie.

Like Uncle Fremont, in *Cause for Wonder,* I came too late for God and too early for the Farm Security Administration. A boy of nine, I left the Platte Valley ignorant of the fact that my home town of Central City had once been called Lone Tree. Neither relates to Lone Tree, the home of Tom Scanlon, and the site of the ceremony in the novel. All of that town is a fiction, an assemblage of roles, parts and missing pieces, saturated with sentiment and reminiscence, brought in at night, under the cover of darkness, and discovered casting real shadows in the morning. Some of this fabrication derived from fiction (over the years I had seen photographs and read frontier journals) but all of it had been processed by the emotion rooted in my boyhood experience. The emotion was what mattered. It would do with the shards of memory all that it could.

When we say, "How well I remember!" we invariably remember rather poorly. It is the emotion that is strong, not the details. The elusive details are incidental, since the emotion is what matters. In this deficiency of memory, in my opinion, we have the origins of the imagination. To repossess we must imagine: our first memories are as dim as they are lasting. Until recorded history, memory constituted history and memory processed by emotion was our only means of repossession. When this is done with appropriate craft we define it as art. Minds differ in the extent they possess the faculty of memory, and how it is processed, but I note in my own certain characteristics that I believe are common to image-making. It is emotion that generates image-making: it is emotion that processes memory. That each artist will process it in his own manner is the hallmark of creative image-making, as distinct from the inventions of fancy. One of the handicaps of science fiction and fantasy is that the image-making is free of the emotion that is characteristic of processed memory, of repossessed life. The mind is often at play, like the summer night buzzing with insects, but to imagine, to make an image, to shape, assemble, and structure, differs from the play of fancy and idle dreaming through the energy it receives from emotion—the degree of this energy is immeasurably low in fiction for "light summer reading."

Image-making begins in earnest where memory fades. The skein of memory is often so frail we see right through it, and it frays at the edges. Invoking its presence is similar to a seance. Is it really *him*, we wonder, or an imposter? Imagination can be lured, but not willed, to do this restoration for us. In good fiction we can usually distinguish those portions that are craftily willed from those winged with imagination. Without the gossamer of memory it is less than life; with it as a ground it proves to be more. First we make these images to see clearly: then we see clearly only what we have made. Over forty years of writing what I have imagined has replaced and overlapped what I once remembered. The fictions have become the facts of my life.

One of our necessary illusions is that we see things as a "whole." If someone says "Look at the wall," and the wall is empty, what we see is blankness. If the wall is a mural, or hung with pictures, or covered with graffiti, the eye must focus on each object separately or see nothing distinctly. We get a "general impression," lacking in details, or we get details without the general impression. A trained eye hopes to get both, as when the critic studies a painting, or the artist studies a landscape, but what we see on the mind's eye of memory is seldom clearly one or the other. An overlapping of many "snapshots," in the manner of a cubistic painting, creates a vibrant or jumbled image that constitutes our impression. The mind is an archive of these sensations. In their infinite variety they surely exhibit individual and general characteristics. Nabokov says, "Speak memory!" but memory is not Hamlet's ghost. It is Nabokov who speaks. On this gauzelike tissue and from these competing fragments the writer chooses and assembles his own pictures. The reader says, "What a memory you have!" but it is what escapes the memory that stirs the imagination.

In the Moldavanka ghetto of Odessa, the child, Isaac Babel, liked to sit under a table, peering out at the world.

As a boy I was given to lying. It was all due to reading. My imagination was always on fire. I read in class, during recess, on the way home, at night—under the dinner table, hidden by the folds of the cloth that reached down to the floor. Reading made me miss all the important doings of this world. *

In these few words light is shed on the subject of fiction and the imagination. Not all writers burn with this fire, but many had their beginnings *under* something. This might be crucial to the act of creation. Far from Odessa, in the Platte Valley of Nebraska, street culverts, piano boxes, storm caves, outhouses, and the dark caves under porches were favored places of concealment. I shared with other small creatures of this world Bre'r Rabbit's instinct to lie low. Seated in dust fine as talcum, my lap a pattern of leaf and slat shadows, I peered out at the world. A train passed, the street darkened with shadows, a tethered cow grazed, sparrows hopped from the wires to the ditch grass, the bell tinkled on the Jewel's Tea Wagon as it rocked on the tracks.

If I see it all clearly, one reason might be that I have so often put it into writing, replacing a vague image with a sharp one. This in turn led to another impression, as I labored at the business of writing. Like the observer of flying objects, I was eager to make clear what seemed so elusive on the mind's eye.

Not long ago I returned to the town I was born in, to the house I associated with my childhood. The porch of this house proved to be a stoop, less than a foot off the ground. A cat might have crawled beneath it, but not a plump child. Other porches were available nearby, but not with the view I had described so clearly. Was I, then, so prematurely a fiction writer?

Referring both to what was written, and what I remembered, I noted other details. The porch was used to store a pair of stilts, a scooter made from a skate, and a Flexible Flyer sled on which I sometimes sat, fizzing soda pop. This Flexible Flyer came late in my boyhood, there being little excuse for it in the flat Platte Valley. Along with the scooter, it came with a porch that sat five steps higher than the sidewalk with adequate sitting room beneath it. Dividing the porch was a swing that creaked and scraped the paint off the house clapboards. A walk curved around the house to the yard at the rear, and seated beneath the porch I would watch the legs pass. A very suitable porch in every way, but in hilly Omaha, and not the Platte Valley.

In the fullness of time I substituted this porch, superior for purposes of observation, for the stoop attached to the house in the Platte Valley. The view was not much, obstructed as it was by the second-floor windows of the neighboring house. When not counting marbles or eating tootsie rolls, I brooded on the life behind the curtained windows. A giant of a man, Mr. Sluzak, lived there with his child-size wife. He drove a big truck for the Railway Express and wore overalls with shoulder straps, like a farmer. His

---

*Isaac Babel, *Benya Krik, The Gangster and Other Stories* (New York: Schocken Books, 1969), p. 65.

daughter, Lillian, showed the tops of her stockings when we played Run Sheep Run under the street light.

If I attempt to distinguish between fiction and memory, and press my nose to memory's glass to see it more clearly, the remembered image grows more immaterial, flickering and insubstantial as reflections on water, or the details of a pointillist painting. The very vividness of the memory is matched by the vagueness of the impression. My recognition is a vibrant fabric of emotion, rippling like silk on which scenes have been painted. These wavering, insubstantial images haunt the memory, they taunt and lure the imagination. If I remembered both vividly and accurately the image-making faculty would be blocked, lacking the need to affirm what is vague or fill in what appears to be empty. Precisely where memory is frail and imperfect, imagination takes fire.

In the clutter of what is remembered and what is imagined some things prove to be symbolic objects. They gather lint. They were in rather than out.

> A bent skate key
> A needle with a burned point
> A ball of tinfoil
> A street car token (found among coins in a
>   city without street cars)
> A gumball machine
> The cracked chimney of a lamp

Artifacts mystically quickened with sentiment and emotion await their reappearance in the imagination, a reenactment and a confirmation. Each time these tokens are handled they give off light.

A few lines back, I was distracted by images embalmed in a fluid of emotion. They came involuntary at the thought, the *image* of, a porch. I had neither seen nor been on it or beneath it for more than fifty years. Now I noted where the chain swing whacked the clapboards, scraping off the paint. I remarked how the breeze stirred the curtains at the window: that the smell of a warming icebox oozed out of the hallways. Behind the screen door a gas jet burned, hissing in its mantle, like a finger held to the lips. Quiet was invoked. The master of the house, who worked nights and slept days, was trying to sleep.

On the dresser in the bedroom, where it ticked loudly, he would put out his railroad watch, on its chain, with the small gold knife that he used to clean the grease from his nails. Until he shaved at the kitchen window where just his lathered head showed above the curtain, he wore his snug whipcord pants with the straps of his braces dangling, his underwear unbuttoned to expose the crinkly hair on his chest. Nothing could have been more commonplace, but it left on Cowie a lasting impression. No ordinary mortal arose so late in the day and

walked around as he did, wearing harness, as if unhitched from the work he had
accomplished while asleep. [One Day, *pp. 76–77*]

I was reluctant to surrender myself to this scene, feeling that I was spying on my own imagination. Unmentioned, but sharp to my senses, is the surrounding presence of a summer morning and the scorched smell of the iron on the draft from the kitchen. In all of this a memory fragment has been processed by emotion—the scorched smell of ironing, the tick of a watch, a lathered face above a half-curtained window—emerging as a new, more gratifying image. An assembly of separate, dispersed impressions, is filtered through a persistent and cherished emotion. The swing creaks, the blind sucks in at the window, water drips in the pan under the icebox.

The American writer, for self-evident reasons, often beginning with the disorder of creation, is "subject to the superstition that objects and places, coherently grouped, disposed for human use and addressed to it, must have a sense of their own, a mystic meaning to give out."

This testimony links Henry James to the object-and-place obsessed imaginations of Whitman and Twain. Image-making exorcises this obsession. A sled by the name of Rosebud, or a similar object, around which sentiment and emotions cluster, waits on the moment that a larger image will provide for its salvage, and release from darkness. How appropriate it is that the fledgling artist tests his faculties on these first impressions. Soon enough he will see more than he remembers, and observe more than he imagines, but the clue to his image-making will be found among the potsherds of his first impressions.

> *When he was a kid he saw the town through a crack in the grain elevator, an*
> *island of trees in the quiet sea of corn. That had been the day the end of the world*
> *was at hand. Miss Baumgartner let them out of school so they could go and*
> *watch it end, or hide and peek at it from somewhere. Dean Cole and him walked*
> *a block and then they ran. They ran all the way to the tracks and down the tracks*
> *to the grain elevator, through a hole in the bottom and up the ladder inside.*
> *They stretched on their bellies and looked through a crack at the town. They*
> *could see all the way to Chapman and a train smoking somewhere. They could*
> *see the Platte beyond the tall corn and the bridge where Peewee had dived in the*
> *sand, and they could see T. B. Horde driving his county fair mare. They could*
> *see it all and the end of the world was at hand.*
> *The end of the world! he said.*
> *HOO-RAY! said Dean Cole.* [The Man Who Was There, *p. 116*]

Memory's chief contribution to this scene was the mood of apprehension and exhilaration, shared with a companion, on hearing this remarkable news. I recall that school was dismissed, a priceless boon well worth the world's loss. Miss Baumgartner was a borrowed detail, as so many were, from my grade school days in Omaha, where I was all of ten years and more observant. I did not go up the ladder, as I reported, since I feared all heights more than humiliation. Peewee and the bridge were a cherished rumor at the time of the writing, but the image was generated by the child's exhilaration at the prospect of a mind-boggling disaster. In this brief fiction I gained a shameful triumph over lost time.

Still earlier, from *The Field of Vision:*

> *That stovepipe came up through the floor from the coke burner in the room below, and where it bulged like a goiter it would get hot when the damper was down. He could hear the coke crackle and settle when he turned it up. . . . All he wanted to do by turning the damper was to bring up the woman who lived below, the way the genie in the picture would rise out of Aladdin's lamp. She would come up with her lamp, the wick swimming in oil, and cross the room like the figures in his dreams, without noises, without so much as taking steps. Holding the lamp to his face she would see that he was asleep. He would feel the heat of the chimney on his forehead, catch a whiff of the oil. She would first open the damper, then turn with the lamp so that the room darkened behind her, but her snow white hair seemed to trap the light. During the day it would be piled on her head, but when she came up with the lamp it would be in braids. With a silver-handled comb that rattled when she used it, facing the mirror that no longer had a handle, she would comb out the tangled ends of her braids. Out would come, like the burrs in a dog's tail, the knotted hairs. When all the hairs stood up, like a brush, she would pass the ends slowly over the chimney where they would curl at the tips and crackle with a frying sound. Then the smell, as when she singed a chicken over a hole in the kitchen range, or turned the bird, slowly, in the flame of a cob dipped in kerosene.* [The Field of Vision, *pp. 106–107*]

It is difficult for me, sixty years after the event, to penetrate the fiction to memory's fading impression. I lie in bed under a sloping ceiling that seems to smoke and waver with looming, hovering shadows, cast by a lamp. Out of my sight a woman hums snatches of hymns, as she brushes her hair. The crackle I hear is made by the brush. It was on another occasion that I saw her test the height of the flame in the chimney by stretching one of her white hairs across the opening at the top. I still fancy I see its burning glow, like the filament in a light bulb. This simple scene has the primal elements that stir both the emotions and the imagination. There is light and darkness, there is mystery, wonder, and a nameless apprehension. The moment is ceremonial. My child's soul is hushed with awe and a tremor of dread as I anticipate her sonorous prayers. If I attempt to recall this actual occasion it blows like smoke, yet something hovers and protects me as if I were cradled at the mouth of a cave. The details are vague, but the emotion is inexhaustible.

To what extent is this true of later events, when the observed details are clearer? In 1958 I visited Mexico, and spent a memorable week in Matamoros. Six years later this experience was the basis of a crucial chapter in *One Day,* published in 1965. A caged bird is a feature of Cowie's experience.

A species of canary, Cowie's first impression had been that it was an object, made of cork and pipe cleaners. Artful, perhaps. No question it was horrible. There were quills, but no feathers, below the neck. The head with its lidded eyes was elevated on the neck like a lampshade. The legs and claws were twisted bits of wire. Cowie took it as an example of the Mexican taste for the macabre: the skull-and-bone cookies eaten by children, the fantastic birds and animals made out of paper. When he glanced up to see it headless, he simply thought the head had dropped off. But no. Nothing lay in the bottom of the cage. The head, with its knife-like beak, had been tucked under the quills of one wing. Fly it could not, lacking the feathers. Sing it would not. But on occasion it hopped. [One Day, p. 180]

Mexico is inexhaustibly exotic, at once exhilarating and harrowing. The sensible and the absurd overlap, the grotesque is commonplace. For the writer, this garden of macabre delights is both an inspiration and a disaster. In admitting to the surreal nature of his impressions, he must maintain the confidence of the sober reader. My own disquieting experience in Matamoros featured a cage without a bird. Gazing at it and through it, over many days and nights, it became for me a memorably symbolic object. In Cowie's circum stance it called for a bird. I imported one I had observed on a previous stay in Queretaro. The perfect setting for both bird and cage were provided by Matamoros. Cowie's Mexican adventure provided the author with the over-view of many previous visits, arresting and insoluble reflections, that arise from the dismaying overlapping of extremes that are both life enhancing and depressing. Without Matamoros none of this would have happened, but little of it actually occurred in Matamoros. The perfect cage had to be found for the imaginary bird.

The proliferating image of our time is the photograph. It is rapidly replac-ing the "abstraction" as the mirror in which we seek our multiple selves. Ironically, it was the photograph that inspired the emergence and triumph of modern art, freeing the imagination of the artist of his obsession with appear-ances. A surfeit of abstractions, and abstracted sensations, a tonic and inspira-tion for half a century, has resulted in a weariness of artifice that the photo-graph seems designed to remedy. What else so instantly confirms our trou-bled sense of the visible world? We need the daily reassurance that it exists. Objects and places, whether coherently grouped or not, constitute the ambi-ence in which we have our being. The photograph confirms, the cinema enshrines "the ineluctable modality of the visible." That includes its abuses, the violence that functions as a pornography of sensation. The film has also obscured, momentarily, that its representations, its imitations of life, is an old rather than a new form of image-making, and that the viewer—by a *com-modius vicus* of recirculation—is back to the startled point of his departure, the need for further image-making. In the dark cave of the theatre, as under the porch, he must re-imagine what it is he thinks he sees.

Speak, memory, but we are not long in doubt as to who it is that speaks.

In this invocation there is a suggestion that memory will speak without intervention. Most writers, as well as readers, would like to think so. It reaffirms our faith in a world that is larger than we are, in a past that truly exists. Are we to accept that memory is the first step in our fiction-making? We do, if the resulting fiction proves to be words. As we now know, language has its own purpose, and distorts in the act of being lucid. To a measurable degree, the more convincing we find the new image the more it has departed from the one remembered. The emotion that fuels the image-making process, and is in turn put to the service of individual talent, departs from the notion that the real world is there to be seized, rather than constructed. It would appear that the primal experience to which God might refer, once we were revealed as naked, and cast out of Eden, is the very experience that is lacking. We are all image-makers, out of necessity. The dreaming cat may have a clearer picture, to his own purpose, than the dreamer in whose lap he curls, but he lacks the faculty of reassembly that distinguishes and terrifies the species homo. Nothing is, but image-making makes it so.

A less sophisticated writer than Nabokov, a frontier plainsman recollecting the frontier experience of his boyhood, dedicates his book to "the most wondrous faculty of memory, God's greatest gift to man."

He is in dead earnest that memory should speak without his willful intervention. He is not disturbed by the problem of transferring memories into language. Confidence of this sort has persuaded most men, including many writers, that memory is an act of repossession free of distortion. No problem arises, in most cases, if the writer is the sole witness to the events described. Here, surely, is the primal experience, rather than one of many wayward impressions. The invention of the photograph gave objective confirmation to the existence of objects, events, and places. We see and document the reality of war. We see planet earth floating above the moon's horizon. This last image is an example of one that exists outside of our abilities to grasp it, in the manner of a religious symbol to which the key emotions are missing.

Before we made fire, before we made tools, we made images. We cannot imagine a time in which we may have lacked imagination. That is what we were, and that is still what we are. In the deep recesses of caves at Lascaux, Altamira, Peche Merle and elsewhere, prehistoric man proved to be an image-maker of baffling sophistication—if we accept the prevalent conception of the pelt-clad primitive of popular science and fiction, a club in one hand, the hair of a female in the other. The ceilings of these caves feature puzzling signs but marvelously clear representations of animals of the hunt. Horses and bisons, the woolly mammoth, the reindeer, are pictured in a manner we think of as "modern." The audacity of the conception is matched by the refinement of execution. Over a gap of twenty thousand years of silence they capture, as we say, our imaginations. We might guess that the artist's talent increased his self-awareness, his sense of uniqueness, distinguishing him from other creatures, this in turn burdening his soul with the enlargement of his sense of wonder. The caves of Lascaux, as well as those near Hannibal, Missouri, in the bluffs along the river, provided refuge for dreamers and image-makers, inscrutably motivated to be more fully conscious. The cave-man, the lunatic, the lover, the poet, and the child under the porch, if we can find one, have at their instant disposal the inexhaustible powers of light and darkness, the ceaseless, commonplace, bewildering commingling of memory, emotion, and imagination. That's where it all comes from. Of the making of such fictions there will not soon be an end.

Faith

When you have done your best, it doesn't matter how good it is. That is for others to say.... An act of the imagination is an act of self-acceptance.... Writing is a way of saying you and the world have a chance.

Richard Hugo

Rainer Maria Rilke   was born in Prague in 1875. He published his first volume of poetry before finishing high school. Best known for the *Duino Elegies* (1923) and *Sonnets to Orpheus* (1923), he has influenced numerous English speaking poets, including W. H. Auden and Robert Lowell. Scholar Robert M. Browning has said that no modern poet "has extended the boundaries of human consciousness through the resources inherent in language as has Rilke." Considered by many to be second only to Goethe, Rilke had published more than a dozen volumes of poetry and fiction by the time of his death in Switzerland in 1926.

From *Letters to a Young Poet*

Rainer Maria Rilke

Paris, February 17th, 1903

My Dear Sir,

Your letter only reached me a few days ago. I want to thank you for its great and kind confidence. I can hardly do more. I cannot go into the nature of your verses; for all critical intention is too far from me. With nothing can one approach a work of art so little as with critical words: they always come down to more or less happy misunderstandings. Things are not all so comprehensible and expressible as one would mostly have us believe; most events are inexpressible, taking place in a realm which no word has ever entered, and more inexpressible than all else are works of art, mysterious existences, the life of which, while ours passes away, endures.

After these prefatory remarks, let me only tell you further that your verses have no individual style, although they do show quiet and hidden beginnings of something personal. I feel this most clearly in the last poem,

Source: *Selections are reprinted from* Letters to a Young Poet *by Rainer Maria Rilke, translated by M. D. Herter Norton, with the permission of W. W. Norton & Company, Inc. Copyright 1934 by W. W. Norton & Company, Inc. Copyright renewed 1962 by M. D. Herter Norton. Revised Edition copyright 1954 by W. W. Norton & Company, Inc.*

"My Soul." There something of your own wants to come through to word and melody. And in the lovely poem "To Leopardi" there does perhaps grow up a sort of kinship with that great solitary man. Nevertheless the poems are not yet anything on their own account, nothing independent, even the last and the one to Leopardi. Your kind letter, which accompanied them, does not fail to make clear to me various shortcomings which I felt in reading your verses without however being able specifically to name them.

You ask whether your verses are good. You ask me. You have asked others before. You send them to magazines. You compare them with other poems, and you are disturbed when certain editors reject your efforts. Now (since you have allowed me to advise you) I beg you to give up all that. You are looking outward, and that above all you should not do now. Nobody can counsel and help you, nobody. There is only one single way. Go into yourself. Search for the reason that bids you write; find out whether it is spreading out its roots in the deepest places of your heart, acknowledge to yourself whether you would have to die if it were denied you to write. This above all—ask yourself in the stillest hour of your night: *must* I write? Delve into yourself for a deep answer. And if this should be affirmative, if you may meet this earnest question with a strong and simple *"I must,"* then build your life according to this necessity; your life even into its most indifferent and slightest hour must be a sign of this urge and a testimony to it. Then draw near to Nature. Then try, like some first human being, to say what you see and experience and love and lose. Do not write love-poems; avoid at first those forms that are too facile and commonplace: they are the most difficult, for it takes a great, fully matured power to give something of your own where good and even excellent traditions come to mind in quantity. Therefore save yourself from these general themes and seek those which your own everyday life offers you; describe your sorrows and desires, passing thoughts and the belief in some sort of beauty—describe all these with loving, quiet, humble sincerity, and use, to express yourself, the things in your environment, the images from your dreams, and the object of your memory. If your daily life seems poor, do not blame it; blame yourself, tell yourself that you are not poet enough to call forth its riches; for to the creator there is no poverty and no poor indifferent place. And even if you were in some prison the walls of which let none of the sounds of the world come to your senses—would you not then still have your childhood, that precious, kingly possession, that treasure-house of memories? Turn your attention thither. Try to raise the submerged sensations of that ample past; your personality will grow more firm, your solitude will widen and will become a dusky dwelling past which the noise of others goes by far away.—And if out of this turning inward, out of this absorption into your own world *verses* come, then it will not occur to you to ask anyone whether they are good *verses.* Nor will you try to interest magazines in your poems: for you will see in them your fond natural possession, a fragment and a voice of your life. A work of art is good if it has sprung from necessity. In this nature of its origin lies the judgment of it: there is no other. Therefore, my dear sir, I know no advice for you save this: to go into yourself and test the deeps in which your life takes rise; at its source you will find the answer to the question whether you *must* create. Accept it, just as it sounds, without inquiring into it. Perhaps it will turn out that you are called to be an artist. Then take that destiny upon yourself and bear it, its burden and its greatness, without ever asking what recompense might come from outside. For the creator must be a world for himself and find everything in himself and in Nature to whom he has attached himself.

But perhaps after this descent into yourself and into your inner solitude you will have to give up becoming a poet; (it is enough, as I have said, to feel that one could live without writing: then one must not attempt it at all). But even then this inward searching which I ask of you will not have been in vain. Your life will in any case find its own ways thence, and that they may be good, rich and wide I wish you more than I can say.

What more shall I say to you? Everything seems to me to have its just emphasis; and after all I do only want to advise you to keep growing quietly and seriously throughout your whole development; you cannot disturb it more rudely than by looking outward and expecting from outside replies to questions that only your inmost feeling in your most hushed hour can perhaps answer.

Viareggio, near Pisa (Italy),
April 5th, 1903

... let me here promptly make a request: read as little as possible of aesthetic criticism—such things are either partisan views, petrified and grown senseless in their lifeless induration, or they are clever quibblings in which today one view wins and tomorrow the opposite. Works of art are of an infinite loneliness and with nothing so little to be reached as with criticism. Only love can grasp and hold and be just toward them. Consider *yourself* and your feeling right everytime with regard to every such argumentation, discussion or introduction; if you are wrong after all, the natural growth of your inner life will lead you slowly and with time to other insights. Leave to your opinions their own quiet undisturbed development, which, like all progress, must come from deep within and cannot be pressed or hurried by anything. *Everything* is gestation and then bringing forth. To let each impression and each germ of a feeling come to completion wholly in itself, in the dark, in the inexpressible, the unconscious, beyond the reach of one's own intelligence, and await with deep humility and patience the birth-hour of a new clarity: that alone is living the artist's life: in understanding as in creating.

There is here no measuring with time, no year matters, and ten years are nothing. Being an artist means, not reckoning and counting, but ripening like the tree which does not force its sap and stands confident in the storms of spring without the fear that after them may come no summer. It does come. But it comes only to the patient, who are there as though eternity lay before them, so unconcernedly still and wide. I learn it daily, learn it with pain to which I am grateful: *patience* is everything!

Viareggio, near Pisa (Italy),
April 23rd, 1903

Here, where an immense country lies about me, over which the winds pass coming from the seas, here I feel that no human being anywhere can answer for you those questions and feelings that deep within them have a life of their own; for even the best err in words when they are meant to mean most delicate and almost inexpressible things. But I believe nevertheless that you will not have to remain without a solution if you will hold to objects that are similar to those from which my eyes now draw refreshment. If you will cling to Nature, to the simple in Nature, to the little things that hardly anyone sees, and that can so unexpectedly become big and beyond measuring; if you have this love of inconsiderable things and seek quite simply, as one who serves, to win the confidence of what seems poor: then everything will become easier, more coherent and somehow more conciliatory for you, not in your intellect, perhaps, which lags marveling behind, but in your inmost consciousness, waking and cognizance. You are so young, so before all beginning, and I want to beg you, as much as I can, dear sir, to be patient toward all that is unsolved in your heart and to try to love the *questions themselves* like locked rooms and like books that are written in a very foreign tongue. Do not now seek the answers, which cannot be given you because you would not be able to live them. And the point is, to live everything. *Live* the questions now. Perhaps you will then gradually, without noticing it, live along some distant day into the answer. Perhaps you do carry within yourself the possibility of shaping and forming as a particularly happy and pure way of living; train yourself to it—but take whatever comes with great trust, and if only it comes out of your own will, out of some need of your inmost being, take it upon yourself and hate nothing.

John Steinbeck   once noted that after completing a book he always felt that he had outgrown what he had to say in it. "I have not written two books alike. For if a writer likes to write, he will find satisfaction in endless experimentation." Steinbeck won the Drama Critic's Circle Award for *Of Mice and Men* (1938), and the Pulitzer Prize for *Grapes of Wrath* (1940), yet he was never popular with academic critics, many of whom were dismayed when he received the Nobel Prize in 1962. The following excerpts were originally written as letters to his friend and editor, Pascal Covici. Each letter was composed in black pencil as a warm-up exercise on the left-hand pages of a large journal. On the right-hand pages, Steinbeck wrote the first draft of *East of Eden*.

From *Journal of a Novel: The East of Eden Letters*

John Steinbeck

The craft or art of writing is the clumsy attempt to find symbols for the wordlessness. In utter loneliness a writer tries to explain the inexplicable. And sometimes if he is very fortunate and if the time is right, a very little of what he is trying to do trickles through—not ever much. And if he is a writer wise enough to know it can't be done, then he is not a writer at all. A good writer always works at the impossible. There is another kind who pulls in his horizons, drops his mind as one lowers rifle sights. And giving up the impossible he gives up writing. Whether fortunate or unfortunate, this has not happened to me. The same blind effort, the straining and puffing go on in me. And always I hope that a little trickles through. This urge dies hard.

Books establish their own pace. This I have found out. As soon as the story starts its style will establish itself. But still I do not think that all the experimenting is wasted that has kept some aliveness.

. . . I will be writing books until I die. But I want to write this one as though it were my last book. Maybe I believe that every book should be written that way. I think I mean that. It is the ideal. And I have done just the opposite. I have written each book as an exercise, as practice for the one to come. And this is the one to come. There is nothing beyond this book—nothing follows it. It must contain all in the world I know and it must have everything in it of which I am capable—all styles, all techniques, all poetry—and it must have in it a great deal of laughter.

It must be told that my second work day is a bust as far as getting into the writing. I suffer as always from the fear of putting down the first line. It is amazing the terrors, the magics, the prayers, the straightening shyness that assails one. It is as though the words were not only indelible but that they spread out like dye in water and color everything around them. A strange and mystic business, writing. Almost no progress has taken place since it was invented. The Book of the Dead is as good and as highly developed as anything in the twentieth century and much better than most. And yet in spite of this lack of a continuing excellence, hundreds of thousands of people are in my shoes—praying feverishly for relief from their word pangs.

And one thing we have lost—the courage to make new words or combinations. Somewhere that old bravado has slipped off into a gangrened scholarship. Oh! you can make words if you enclose them in quotation marks. This indicates that it is dialect and cute.

I have a weary little weight on my head today. Last night I could not sleep out of excitement about my story. It was a strange voluptuous excitement and when I dropped off I had a quick sex dream, perhaps because my feeling was exotic. Now I am slipping so far ahead of the pages for narrative but there's no harm in that. I have said to myself that this book must be unhurried and serene. And if these observations can promote the calm I want, then I am willing to go along with it indefinitely. I am pleased with myself for no reason at all. I have a good golden light in my stomach which is a mesh of happiness. Isn't that odd and delightful? Every once in a while I get the feeling that this is a secret book like some of the others that were kept in a gloom and burned straight, and a good thing too for they carried uncreative misery and there is no good in that at all. How different now—maybe I'm fooling myself. That is always possible but I do indeed seem to feel creative juices rushing toward an outlet as semen gathers from the four quarters of a man and fights its way into the vesicle. I hope something beautiful and true comes out—but this I know (and the likeness to coition still holds). Even if I knew nothing would emerge from this book I would still write it. It seems to me that different organisms must have their separate ways of symbolizing, with sound or gesture, the creative joy—the flowering. And if this is so, men also must have their separate ways—some to laugh and some to build, some to destroy and yes, some even creatively to destroy themselves. There's no explaining this. The joy thing in me has two outlets: one a fine charge of love toward the incredibly desirable body and sweetness of woman, and second—mostly both—the paper and pencil or pen. And it is interesting to think what paper and pencil and the wriggling words are. They are nothing but the trigger into joy—the shout of beauty—the cacajada of the pure bliss of creation. And often the words do not even parallel the feeling except some-times in intensity. Thus a man full of a bursting joy may write with force and vehemence of some sad picture—of the death of beauty or the destruction of a lovely town—and there is only the effectiveness to prove how great and beautiful was his feeling.

You might as well get used to this, Pat. I write many thousands of words a day and some of them go on paper. And of those which are written down, only a few are ever meant to be seen.

In this connection—I can find in notebooks many years old ideas and feelings and even stories I did not know about. For this reason it is not well to attempt to analyze too closely at first—an emotion which falls by some acci-dent into edged words, swings the whole brain about and shakes it like a rug. This happens oftener than we know.

I feel that sometimes when I am writing I am very near to a kind of unconsciousness. Then time does change its manner and minutes disappear into the cloud of time which is one thing, having only one duration. I have thought that if we could put off our duration-preoccupied minds, it might be that time has no duration at all. Then all history and all pre-history might indeed be one durationless flash like an exploding star, eternal and without duration.

Just as it always does—the work started without warning. It is always that way. I must sit a certain length of time before it happens. Yesterday it began to come and I think the form is set now. I know it is for the alternate chapters. I only hope I can do as well with the other parts of the alternate. Now I have sat a week. It is Friday and I have sweated out one page and a half. If I did not know this process so well, I would consider it a week of waste. But I know better than that now and I am content. I do not think I have wasted this week.

I went to work so early this morning that it is still early. And I could go on and do some more work. But I think the energy core is kind of worn down. I think, since I have done so much so far, that I will let it go for the day. I don't want to get too tired. I want to take enough time so that I will avoid the rather terrible exhaustion of the Grapes of Wrath. I'll tell you one thing though—although this book is more subtle and perhaps less emotional in an obvious way, it is going to be more peopled than the Grapes. We are going to meet—try to know and move on from—one hell of a lot of people. Since in these work notes I am putting down everything freely, I can give you an example of what I mean when I say the book is really beginning to move and breathe and have a life of its own. I had thought to set Carl Trask and his wife in perhaps three paragraphs. But then I got fascinated with him, not only as a character but with his character as a mover and shaper even if in reverse so that his effect comes moving down the generations. I thought he was going to have only one wife and I find he has two. I thought he was an only child and he has a half brother. I thought to bring him right into the Salinas Valley and now I doubt whether he will get there in under twenty-five pages. I guess that's what I mean by the book taking its own pace and almost thinking for itself.

. . . a story has a life of its own. It must be allowed to take its own pace. It can't be pushed too much. If it is, the warp shows through and the story is unnatural and unsafe. And this story of mine must be safe. At last I wonder how many events are accidents and how many are created and forced by the natures of the protagonists. To a large extent I lean toward the latter.

I should easily finish this chapter today. There isn't a great deal more of it. Yesterday the symbolic killing of brother by brother. I have only the recruiting and the last night with Alice visiting perhaps. But I have other things too. I want to wind this first chapter up well. The others are not so clear cut. But I like a chapter to have design of tone, as well as of form. A chapter should be a perfect cell in the whole book and should almost be able to stand alone. If this is done then the breaks we call chapters are not arbitrary but rather articulations which allow the free movement of the story. I think you will find that the theme is beginning to emerge. And it had to take time. It will emerge again and again. But this time it will just peer out and withdraw.

A symbol is usually a kind of part of an equation—it is one part or facet chosen to illuminate as well as to illustrate the whole. The symbol is never the whole. It is a kind of psychological sign language. But in this book, which I want to have a semblance of real experience both visual and emotional and finally intellectual, I want to clothe my symbol people in the trappings of experience so that the symbol is discernible but not overwhelming.

You know I am really stupid. For years I have looked for the perfect pencil. I have found very good ones but never the perfect one. And all the time it was not the pencils but me. A pencil that is all right some days is no good another day. For example, yesterday, I used a special pencil soft and fine and it floated over the paper just wonderfully. So this morning I try the same kind. And they crack on me. Points break and all hell is let loose. This is the day when I am stabbing the paper. So today I need a harder pencil at least for a while. I am using some that are numbered 2⅜. I have my plastic tray you know and in it three kinds of pencils for hard writing days and soft writing days. Only sometimes it changes in the middle of the day, but at least I am equipped for it. I have also some super soft pencils which I do not use very often because I must feel as delicate as a rose petal to use them. And I am not often that way. But when I do have such moments I am prepared. It is always well to be prepared. Pencils are a great expense to me and I hope you know it. I buy them four dozen at a time. When in my normal writing position the metal of the pencil eraser touches my hand, I retire that pencil. Then Tom and Catbird get them. And they need pencils. They need lots of pencils. Then I have this kind of pencil and it is too soft. *Whenever you see a thing like that, the point broke. I have fine prejudices, lazy ones and enjoyable ones. It occurs to me that everyone likes or wants to be an eccentric and this is my eccentricity, my pencil trifling. It isn't a very harmful one.

I wonder why, on such a day as this, when the story is particularly clear in my head, I have a kind of virginal reluctance to get to it. I seem to want to think about it and moon about it for a very long time before I actually get down to it. Today, I think I know one of the main reasons. Today's work is so important that I am afraid of it. It requires the use of the most subtle rhythms both of speech and thought. And I use that last advisedly because thought has its rhythms and qualities just as poetry has. I think that the two are very closely related. Thus after a couple of days off, I think I write in this page almost like a pitcher warming up to pitch—getting my mental arm in shape to pitch a good game. And the pitcher is not a bad symbol since he must have smoothness and coordination and rhythm all together.

It took three years of puzzled thinking to work out this plan for a book. Believe me, today I am not putting off work. In fact it is nudging me to get to it but I do want to set these things down.

A book comes in fits and jerks, Pat. Actual wordage on S.V.* started Feb. 15. It made very good progress for quite a long time, in fact until last Thursday. Then you came over and took the first part for typing. Now I don't know whether there is any connection but right then I went into a tail spin. The next three days, through Sunday, I went into a depression that was devastating. I do not think it was because of taking away the mss., but the whole thing is such a delicate matter that I just don't know. What I do know is that it was very painful, hard on me and perhaps harder on Elaine. Now it is Monday and I am all weak and shaken. I am forced to lift myself out of the despondency by the bootstraps. And I will.

I want to ask and even beg one thing of you—that we do not discuss the book any more when you come over. No matter how delicately we go about it, it confuses me and throws me off the story. So from now on let's do the weather or fleas or something else but let's leave the book alone. In that way we'll have some surprises. I know you won't mind this once you see why. Once it is done, you may tear it to shreds if you wish and I won't object, and I'll go along with you, but right now both you and I forget the delicate sets of balances involved. There are no good collaborations and all this discussion amounts to collaboration. So, we'll do that, if you don't mind. And let's stop counting pages, too. I am not being difficult I hope. It is just too hard on me to try to write, defend and criticize all at the same time. I can quite easily do each

---

*"The Salinas Valley" had been the working title from the beginning.

one separately. Let me keep the literary discussions on these poor pages. Then we will have no quarrels.

Yesterday I felt weak and frightened at the thought of Part II. But today all that is gone and only a good calmness has taken its place. Perhaps that is because yesterday I thought of it as an immense whole and today my mind is on its opening.

I thought about the book a great deal yesterday—what it is about and what its title should be. It is not local. It is not primarily about the Salinas Valley nor local people. Therefore it should have a general title. Now—its framework roots from that powerful, profound and perplexing story in Genesis of Cain and Abel. There is much of it that I don't understand. Furthermore it is very short, but this story with its implications has made a deeper mark in people than any other save possibly the story of the Tree of Life and original sin. Now since this is indeed my frame—is there any reason to conceal it from my reader? Would it not be better to let him know even in the title what the story is about? With this in mind I went back to Genesis. I do not want a direct quotation but if I can find a symbol there which is understood on sight and which strikes deep, I will have my title. The punishment of Cain is a strange and perplexing one. Out of Eve's sin came love and death. Cain invented murder and he is punished by life and protection. The mark put on him is not placed there to punish him but to protect him. Have you ever thought of that? And this is the best known mark in the world. So I suggest as a title for my book Cain Sign. It is not a direct quote, it is short, harsh, memorable and nearly everyone in the world knows what it means. And it is pretty good-looking title too. What do you think of it?

I wish I knew how people do good and long-sustained work and still keep all kinds of other lives going—social, economic, etc. I can't. I seem to have to waste time, so much dawdling to so much work. I am frightened by this week before it even happens. If I had any sense I would leave my book this week. But that would not be good because it would take too long to come back to it. So I'll simply get as much done as I can and work as long as is feasible.

And now I had set down in my own hand the 16 verses of Cain and Abel and the story changes with flashing lights when you write it down. And I think I have a title at last, a beautiful title, EAST OF EDEN. And read the 16th verse to find it. And the Salinas Valley is surely East of Eden. I could go on and write another page and perhaps it would be good, who knows. Or maybe not. What a strange story it is and how it haunts one. I have dreaded getting into this section because I knew what the complications were likely to be. And they weren't less but more because as I went into the story more deeply I began to realize that without this story—or rather a sense of it—psychiatrists would have nothing to do. In other words this one story is the basis of all human neurosis—and if you take the fall along with it, you have the total of the psychic troubles that can happen to a human. I am not going to write any more today but maybe tomorrow I can do a little more.

Now tomorrow I will have a final statement of my theme and it will never again be mentioned in the book. With the death of Samuel the whole tempo of the book is going to change just as the tempo of the times changed. It will speed and rage then. You'll see. I manage to stay excited about this book. It has never been dull to me. I hope it will not be for other people. I feel both humble and proud about this book. It's an odd feeling. I've never felt quite so about anything of mine. I'm trying to write the microcosm. I have a little feeling that I am succeeding. Some of tomorrow's work is going to be very funny, I think. A really amusing venture in scholarship. But I must leave space for certain words which I have asked you to give me. I'll fill the word in later together with the definition you will find for me. And that is all for today and I am satisfied with today's work.

One is never drained by work but only by idleness. Lack of work is the most enervating thing in the world.

You would be interested in my fingers, I think. I have designed pieces of rubber bandage to protect them from the pencil. They are so beat up that they hurt but my new method works fine.

In the evening I am doing a little wood carving while listening to bad radio music. I have tried to read but I find I don't pay any attention to the script of the book because I am always thinking of my own. A real monomaniac.

Let me inspect then the book itself. It must be nearly 500 pages by now. It started by saying, "I'm going to tell you how things were then." Now, has it done that? I don't know. I just don't know. It left customs and clothes and habits and went deeply into people but I think that is very good rather than bad. For customs are only the frame for people. You can't write a book about customs unless it is a treatise. And I don't want a treatise. I want the participation of my reader. I want him to be so involved that it will be his story. You are tied up in this story very deeply. I doubt whether you can see what has been accomplished because, through these notes, you know what the intention is. And perhaps because you know what was intended, you may believe that it has been accomplished. To that extent, these notes may be bad. I don't know.

Today, the work is bound to be slow. All week end I thought about it. The new section is about to start. It is a change in time, a change in direction. The nation, the Valley are changing their direction and also their tempo. How am I going to indicate this? I don't know. I want to keep the curious relaxed feeling. Maybe the best way will be simply to tell the truth about it. Maybe the hardest thing in writing is simply to tell the truth about things as we see them. That might be so. I have surely tried to do that in this book. I would hate to lose it in literary trickery now.

This is a time of great joy. It will never be so good again—never. A book finished, published, read—is always an anticlimax to me. The joy comes in the words going down and the rhythms crowding in the chest and pulsing to get out.

If I were not so nearly finished with this volume, I would not permit myself the indiscipline of overwork. This is the falsest of economies. But since end is in view I am permitting myself the indulgence. It is two o'clock in the morning and I can't stay away from my book. Since I can't sleep anyway I might just as well be putting words down instead of only thinking them.

So, we go into the last week and I may say I am very much frightened. I guess it would be hard to be otherwise—all of these months and years aimed in one direction and suddenly it is over and it seems that the thunder has produced a mouse.

Last week there was complete exhaustion and very near collapse. I guess to anyone who has not worked in this way it would be hard to conceive this kind of slow accumulated weariness. I don't know any other work that requires month after month of emotional as well as intellectual concentration, although there may be some. I'm glad I took three days off. I slept a drugged sleep most of the time, and one without drugs. Wouldn't say I am much rested but I think I have the energy to finish at least.

You must be no less frightened than I because you don't know what is going to happen and all I don't know is whether I can make it happen. So in a way I am better off than you are. It is too bad we have not more humor about this. After all it is only a book and no worlds are made or destroyed by it. But it becomes important out of all proportion to its importance. And I suppose that is essential. The dunghill beetle must be convinced of the essential quality in rolling his ball of dung, and a golfer will not be any good at it unless striking a little ball is the most important thing in the world. So I must be convinced that this book is a pretty rare event and I must have little humor about it. Can't afford to have. The story has to move on and on and on. It is like a machine now—set to do certain things. And it is about to clank to its end.

And I might just as well get to it because putting it off isn't going to help a bit.

Robert Crichton is best known for *The Great Imposter* (1959) and *The Secret of Santa Vittoria* (1961), both of which were made into successful films. Born of parents who were writers in New Mexico, Crichton has been a professional writer, journalist, and editor all his life. "I continue to maintain," he says, "that telling a story to convey feeling and experience is . . . as natural to man and as vital to man, and as intuitive and ageless . . . as to embrace when in love and to flee when in fear." Crichton's last novel, *The Camerons,* was published in 1972; he is currently working on a novel drawn from his World War II experiences.

Across the River and into the Prose

Robert Crichton

The only thing I ever wanted to accomplish in life was to write a good novel. I wanted this so much that I came to think of myself as being a novelist even though I had never written one. Despite this little failing I was quite convinced that were I to die right then my obituary would read Crichton, Novelist, Writes Last Chapter because everyone would know how much it meant to me. And it would only be fair; I had all the novels in my head. All that was lacking was the technical formality of transferring them to paper.

This state of affairs went on until I was past thirty. When no novel had appeared, in order to account for the void and save my self-respect, I was driven to conclude that I was a classic example of the pitfalls of Grub Street. I was a free-lance magazine writer then, living from one assignment to the next, always one advance behind, and I saw myself as a victim of the literary sharecropper system, as hopelessly snared in my web of circumstances as those wretched cotton farmers James Agee described in *Let Us Now Praise Famous Men.*

The matter was out of my hands. I was a victim and I was quite happy that way until the spring of 1962 when a magazine publisher named Henry Steeger came back from a lunch he had with some Italian wine growers and told me the story of a small Italian hill town where the people had hidden

Source: Reprinted by permission of Curtis Brown, Ltd. Copyright © 1969 by Harper & Row, Publishers, Inc.

1,000,000 bottles of wine from the Germans and how they managed to keep their enormous secret.

"Someone should write that," Mr. Steeger said. "It has the quality of legend and yet it happened in our own time."

I could recognize that much. I was astonished in fact that this fat plum of a story, swelling with possibilities, was still unplucked. By this time, however, I had so perfected my defenses to repel anything that even hinted at the potential of becoming a novel that I was able to tell myself that it actually wasn't a very good story at all. I increasingly found it more desirable to apologize for a book I hadn't written (but which just might be great) than to apologize for one I had written.

Camus has written that ultimately all men are prey to their truths, even in the act of denying them, and Santa Vittoria became one of mine. Even while denying it I knew the story of this town was the basis for a big grab bag of a novel, a *bildungs-roman,* in which, because of the sprawling framework of the story, almost anything goes and anything works. Against my will the story preyed upon me, fermenting in my doughy spirit, fizzing there like a cake of yeast in a wine vat.

I woke one morning in March, there was snow and thunder in the morning, very rare and very strange, with the line "In dreams begin responsibilities" running in my mind. It is a line from Yeats (borrowed, I have since found out, from some obscure Indian poet) that I used to write in all my notebooks when I was in college. It is a line that has been the subject of profound scrutiny and some subtle interpretations have resulted from it. But on this morning the line was very clear to me: If you dream about something all the time you have a responsibility to do something about it. I apologize to William Butler Yeats. I began going around New York that morning trying to raise enough money to take me to Italy. I felt the least I could do was look at this place which had become my responsibility. When I accumulated $800 beyond the cost of a round-trip air fare I set out for Santa Vittoria.

The trip to Italy, which by any other terms than those of a writer would have to be classed as a continuous disaster, I include here because it illustrates something important about the craft, namely, anything that happens to a writer can, with good fortune, be turned into something of value. In a matter of weeks I was run down by a car in Rome, robbed in a country inn, and managed to make a profound fool of myself in Santa Vittoria, and each incident turned out to be more fortunate than the one before it.

The car incident is a good example. I was in a pedestrian crosswalk which guaranteed me the right of way when the car bore down on me. I, an American and a believer in the sanctity of signs, couldn't believe he was going to keep on coming. He couldn't believe I wasn't going to jump out of the way. He must have been a good driver because he only drove halfway over my body before managing to stop. I had my first intimation of the way things were going to go when a man helped me out from under the car.

"You're very lucky," he said. "You didn't dent the fender."

My last intimation, or my first revelation, of truth came in the police station. I was talking about justice and my rights and I could see that they felt I was not well balanced. I didn't get the idea, they assured me. The car was bigger and faster and stronger than me and therefore the car had the right of way. Couldn't I see that much?

So on only my second day in Italy I was privileged to begin to understand the basic fact of Italian life which is that power, the balance of it, the having and not having it, is the key to all life. Survival depends on a respect for it. The possession or lack of it determines the course of a man's existence. Success depends on how well you learn to manipulate it. I was never able to get anyone in Italy to be sympathetic about being run down in a safety zone. They would listen to the story and they would nod and then they would always say: "Yes, but why *didn't* you jump out of the way?"

These people, then, who pass themselves off to the world and to themselves as romantics are the most realistic of people. Two broken fingers and the knees gone from the pants of my one good suit was a small price to pay for such knowledge. I might have spent months in Italy before learning what I did.

The robbery was a very Italian kind of crime. I was headed north to Santa Vittoria, taking all the back roads available so I would have a feel of the country before getting there, and I took a room in a country inn on the second floor with a terrace. Few Italians would have taken that room. It faced away from the inn and not in toward the courtyard. Italians like to be with people. Americans, who have allowed the North European psyche to inflict itself upon our national soul, prefer privacy. Even if he took the room no Italian would have then opened the window on to the terrace. They don't trust the night air and what might come in with it. Americans like to clean the portals of the mind with fresh night air and they like to be trusting and believe in the possibilities for humankind to be good.

It must have looked like a ritual scene from some old Italian *novella*. The thief came up the stone wall at night and onto the terrace and into the room and through my pockets. I should still be angry with him but the thief did one marvelous thing; he left me half of my money. I picture him working swiftly and dangerously in the dark to leave me my share and I warm to him. He was a humanist and a man generous to strangers which is as good a definition of a gentleman as any. So another factor; Life is a matter of power tempered by an incorruptible humanity, which in itself is a kind of power. I was a more tolerant man after that and I was also one long step down toward poverty and my ultimate entry into the Italian lower depths where few outsiders are allowed to go.

In Santa Vittoria, on my first day, I was invited to a luncheon at the winery held for some American wine buyers and I proceeded first to praise and then to rave about one particular wine which I assured those present made all the rest taste like scented toilet water. Certainly someone should have warned me that the wine I was praising was a comparison wine, designed to make the local wines taste good by comparison. It was suggested by a company official after the lunch that I didn't seem to be the right man to tell the story of the great thing they did in Santa Vittoria. I left the town the same day I arrived in it.

And this was fortunate, too. Fearful of attempting a novel I had determined to write a non-fiction book but now I had no alternative. I also thought that I would be able to live off the generosity of the people I was writing about and now I was condemned to live off the land. I headed south, down the spine of the Apennines, in search of my own Santa Vittoria. In all I stayed in twenty hill towns, each one separate in my mind and yet all of them finally merging into one conglomerate city, richer than the sum of its parts. I learned some things of value along the way.

In the beginning I had the belief that people would resent my intrusion and I sat at solitary tables in the cafe in the piazza and sat like Proust at a party, "*J'observe, j'observe.*" It took me time to learn that my discretion only bred suspicion. No one told me anything honest. At last I fell back on the tactic of simple honesty. On arriving in a new town I learned to approach the first person who seemed to command respect and tell him exactly what I was doing in his town. I was an American, a writer, I was planning a book on just such a town as this one, but not this one, and I wanted to know everything good and everything bad about life in a hill town that anyone wanted to tell me. Very often the man would take me to the mayor who would tell me everything good about the town and then the people would come and tell me everything bad about it.

Every day I grew poorer and this was good since it put me into the hands and then the homes of people I couldn't have met otherwise. Toward the end of my stay I was reduced to knocking on stranger's doors and asking if they would like to sell me a plate of peas and rice or some soup and bread and wine for 100 *lire*. They were always happy to do it. Someone could always go without a meal but where could they get an extra 100 *lire*? I learned a great many things with my soup.

The trouble with poverty as a tactic is that you can't fake it. I don't think you can plan to be poor and in this way get to meet what are always referred to as the people. I tried it afterwards in Appalachia and in the coal fields of Scotland and it was no good. Peasants smell the poverty in you. When you pay the 100 *lire* you have to feel the sweat on your forehead as you count the money out. And you have to do sneaky little things to save little sums of money that peasants recognize but which the bourgeoisie never even notice.

There is little to do in hill towns after dark and because of it, the loneliness, I developed a system of information gathering that has proved invaluable to me since. From a simple need to communicate, with no specific purpose in mind, I began to write long rambling letters home, putting down everything that interested me or puzzled me during the day. Months later, when I sat down to start on the first draft of *Santa Vittoria*, it was the letters that turned out to be filled with the kind of information I needed. My notes were mostly useless.

The reason for this, I think, is that a letter is an inclusive thing. Notes tend to be selective and therefore exclusive. When a person is taking notes he generally has some idea of what he is looking for. The haphazard, the irrelevant, the unexpected, since it doesn't fit the pattern is ignored or not even seen. I suppose it is possible to do as well by keeping a diary as writing a letter but most people tend to cheat in diaries. As time passes entries tend to become more terse and cryptic, the diary becomes filled with one-line notations the writer is sure he will be able to re-create later, with all the emotion and sounds and smells. In a letter, since it is going to someone else, the effort to re-create has to be made right then if the letter is going to make any sense at all. It's more interesting to write to someone else than oneself anyway. The only people who write good diaries are people who know their logs will be part of history and egoists who hope theirs will be.

When I returned from Italy I attempted to organize my notes because this is what I felt writers did. The notes were so meagre and pointless, however, I began making notes from the letters. These I put in a large shoebox because I couldn't think of any sensible way to file them. It was sloppy and disorganized and yet the system had an unexpected virtue to it. In order to find out something I was compelled to flip through as many as a hundred notes and while doing this I was reminded of all kinds of facets of Italian life that I wouldn't have remembered if I had been able to go to the source at once. Some of this haphazard extraneous information was bound to seep into the scene I was working on and the scene would be a little richer for it. In time I came to think of the shoebox as my compost pile, a dung heap for potential fertility, and the leaping from note to note as an act of cross-fertilization. Marianne Moore once wrote something close to "Thank God for the privilege of disorganized things" and in this case she is right.

I kept making notes because I was afraid to actually start the book. For the same reason, to avoid starting, I began to read a great deal about Italy, hill towns, wine making, despite the fact that I had been led to believe that it wasn't a good idea for a novelist to read too much about the subject he would be writing about. The idea was that the reading tended to rob the writer of his individuality and that he would be exposed to material similar to his own and would not want to use it although he might actually handle it in quite a different fashion. There is also always the danger of reading something so superlative that the writer will be smothered by it. Who wants to write a novel about the War of 1812 after reading *War and Peace?* In my case, while admittedly stalling, the reading turned out to be enormously rewarding. Everything I read seemed to trigger some kind of creative response in me. It didn't matter very much what the subject was or whether the writing was good or bad, anything at all I read had the potential to give birth to an idea, often one that had no relationship with the reading at all. Some African tribes believe that energy creates energy and it got this way with my reading; every response seemed to create climate for a heightened response. One of what I will boldly call the more effective scenes in *Santa Vittoria*, a competitive dance in a wine press, was suggested to me by a series of letters from an Edwardian schoolteacher to her class while on vacation in Sicily. She thought the wine pressers were ugly because they looked like hairy pagan goats. One incident, which plays an important part in the book, occurred to me while reading the financial statement of a modern wine company. When the barometer of the creative nature is set for a spell of writing, evidently anything can excite it and in my experience, and to my surprise, reading had the strongest potential of all.

There finally came a time when I could no longer find a believable excuse not to begin. I even announced the fact to my family and friends. "Tomorrow, I begin." I made it easy on myself. I vowed I would write exactly one page and write just one page for a week. This shouldn't frighten anyone and at the end of the week I would be like a colt let out to his first pasture.

But I couldn't do it. All day I sat at my desk and I wrote one word. "If." Toward evening I wrote the word in pencil so that it covered the entire page. The next day I wrote "So now I begin" and never got further than that. The day after that I tried the reliable weather and date technique. "On a cold blustery morning in May, 1943, on the sunless eastern slopes of the Apennines, spring was coming hard. . . ."

After that I quit. I rented an office away from home not to inspire creativity but to hide me from those who could see me doing nothing for hours on end. I gave up the idea of one page; this goal seemed insurmountable. I came under the idea that if I could get one good opening sentence, the keynote, and get it down right, the rest of the book would unravel itself from there. I was very conscious of the fact that I was like the man in Camus' *The Plague* who spends thirty years on *his* opening sentence, honing it, pruning it, polishing it, but it didn't matter. Who was to say if he got his sentence right the rest of his book wouldn't have inevitably followed. It was all I had to hang on to.

"How did it go today?" my wife would ask.

"It's coming; it's coming," followed by several very strong drinks.

One afternoon I realized I was never going to write the sentence and once I understood that I arrived at the idea of disowning art. I had become so self-conscious about style and craft that I had become incapable of reading or hearing words any longer. When I said them they sounded strange and when I put them down on paper they looked strange. I recall writing "This book begins" and then stopping because the word book looked wrong. What kind of word was book. An indefinite word. It could be a checkbook or the Bible. Volume was better. Journal even better. "This journal begins. . . ." Too pompous. But I couldn't go back to book. Novel, that was the real, precise word I wanted. But what kind of novel? The reader had a right to know.

In this way the day went. It was possible to fill a wastebasket in a day and never write over four different words. I always used a clean fresh sheet for a clean fresh start. With every empty sheet there was hope, and failure. On this afternoon, however, I began to write the story of Santa Vittoria in the form and style of a Dick and Jane first reader.

"There is a little town on a hill called Santa Vittoria. It is in Italy. The people in the town grow grapes and make wine. A great thing took place in the town. One day, not too long ago. . . ."

It astonishes me now that I was able to keep this up for several weeks. Because the words didn't count the words poured out. And I was happy about the sound of my typewriter because I had grown embarrassed by the silence from my cubicle.

"What's he do?"

"He's a writer."

"Oh. What's he write?"

"I don't know. I never heard him write."

I heard that. Now the pages were piling up and I felt good. It was silly, considering the manuscript was one that I would have shot someone over, before allowing him to see it, and yet the feeling was real. In the end I had several hundred pages filled with one-syllable words and while I pretended to disown the pile of paper it meant a great deal to me. It was no good but at last I had *something* which was no good. All kinds of things were missing but now they were missing from something. I was conscious that through Dick and Jane I had outflanked art.

A week later I cut the manuscript down to 125 pages and in the process something strange happened to it. In the starkness of its naked simplicity the book became mysterious in tone. In the cutting the manuscript had become fragmented into a series of pared-to-the-bone pastiches and I was faced with the realization that somehow, inadvertently, I seemed to have written A New Novel. I had the wild thought that Alain Robbe-Grillet would discover me. The book would be published by Grove Press and reviewed by *The New York Review of Books,* perhaps (who could tell how far it might go) by Susan Sontag, favorably, of course, thereby immortalizing me to my peer group; and then the thought passed. I was a fraud and what could be more fraudulent among the grapes and stones and lives of Santa Vittoria than a novel Alain Robbe-Grillet could approve of? Marienbad, *oui,* Santa Vittoria, *non.*

I had the bones of a book. The problem now was to flesh out the skeleton. I was still afraid to begin but not as much as before. The first act of creation is the terrifying thing and once this is done, it now seems to me, no matter how badly, something menacing has been overcome. I wasn't swimming yet but I was in the water.

I began by putting *place* in the book. I wanted a sense of the town to permeate the book because place plays such an important part in the book. What happened could only happen in an isolated hill town. Whenever there was a change of scene I began to describe in detail what the new place would look like, whether it was a room, the piazza, the entire town itself. In this process of supplying place the absence of people to the place made itself evident. Almost in spite of myself I began to people the places and in this way the book began to get itself written.

I have never had any idea about character. It is one reason I don't think I could teach literature. I only seem to see what people do. I don't recognize an evil man until he does something evil and then I'm not sure that he meant it to be evil. The same goes for good people. There is no good or evil in itself, as Camus has pointed out, but only the consequences of acts. All things are in all people at all times. So I couldn't plot out a character or even conceive of one, they simply happen, and from day to day, capable of a ridiculous, mean action one day and something generous the very next day.

"The character lacks unity." What nonsense. "He wouldn't have done that." What nonsense. He *did* it. Everyone is ultimately capable of almost everything which is after all the fascination and horror of life.

In his book *Individuals*, P. F. Strawson has written that "the primary conceptual scheme must be one that puts people in the world. A conceptual scheme which puts a world in each person must be, at least, a secondary product."

This idea is one of the few dogmas about writing that I am conscious of holding. I didn't want my characters to stand for anything, to explain, to symbolize, to account for anything but simply, in the words of Denis Donaghue when describing what a novel should be, possessed of life to a degree of irrelevance . . . all carelessness and luck, who, when given their first push, would leap on their way.

My final concern was style, although I didn't know it then. I am ashamed to admit that I thought of style as a mannerism, the decor of a book. I learned later that this is a technique, an artifice, not a style. The best description of style I have ever read and one of the most valuable lines about writing is by the same Donaghue who says: Style is the right feeling animating the voice.

I had no voice. I didn't know who was telling the story and why he was telling it. If I chose a Santa Vittorian I would be compelled to accept the limitations of a peasant's vision of life. I could choose to be the author as God, omniscient, wilful, intolerant, irrational, as gods tend to be, but I knew I didn't function well as God. It's not my type. One day I thought of an Italian writing a novel about life in Conway, Arkansas, and I almost fell apart. The opportunities for error were endless. As a result my decision was made for me. I was forced into what might be called a literary cop-out but which became inevitable. To account for my ignorance I invented as narrator an Italian-American airman, a deserter who parachutes from his plane after a pointless bombing of a nearby hill town and who has remained in Santa Vittoria after the war because of his fear of returning and a misguided sense of shame about what he did. He hopes that by telling this story he can earn some money and by explaining why he deserted in one part of the book, in exchange for telling the greater story, perhaps redeem himself.

Was it the proper voice? Does it meet Donaghue's criteria? Probably not. In the long haul the narrator is not truly a voice but a device and not a character (he mercifully almost never appears in the book) but a sound. The worst part of it for me was that I didn't commit the errors that I was certain I would. So I didn't need Robert Abruzzi after all but I didn't know it then and that was important. He served me well but let him know this: If Abruzzi were to come back to Santa Vittoria again I would have him lined up against a wall and edited to death.

When I had written 150 pages through the eyes of Abruzzi I sent what I had done to my publisher, Simon and Schuster, in the hope of getting an advance. Unfinished manuscripts tend to seem more promising to editors, I was told. Also, if the publisher gives an advance he now has a vested interest in the final product. An advance tends to blind an editor's judgement of a manuscript since the house is already committed. Finally the advance is supposed to bolster the unsure writer's confidence.

"They really *want* me. They *believe* in me."

None of it worked this way for me. I did nothing until I got the advance and when I did it had the effect of stopping me altogether. Now there was no way out. I had taken the money and I was the one who was committed. I had a contract. They could take me to court if I didn't produce a novel. But perhaps it was all to the best. I determined not to spend the money, but I did, and it was finally my fear of having to pay the money back, which grew stronger than my fear of failure, which led me to finish the book. It was this version the publisher bought.

I felt they were wrong to buy it. I knew the book was all wrong. I had the place I wanted in the book and the people and the story but each of these elements stood in its own place, one immovable chunk of writing hard by another. The novel seemed to me like a freshly blasted quarry with no one to pick up the pieces. By chance I saw an editor's note about the book that said: "This is really very good you know" and I felt the note was a plant, a kind of editor's waterwings designed to buoy me up for the sea of revisions ahead.

They asked for very few revisions and this I took as a very bad sign. If they were really interested in the book they would want all kinds of changes. I figured they had given up on the book but would go ahead and print it in the hopes of recovering their advance. They gave me two weeks to make the revisions we agreed to. One of them was on page one, a four letter word which wasn't called for but which I had included to show right off that I wasn't afraid to use four letter words. I scratched the word out and the page looked messy and so I retyped it and it came out a line short so I retyped the second page and it came out wrong so I went on to the third page. I began cutting some paragraphs and then an entire scene and to add dialogue and change dialogue and somewhere along the way that morning a new character entered the story. I had meant to work until lunch but when I stopped I was surprised to find that it was five o'clock in the afternoon and I had written 42 pages. I had no sensation of having worked hard. I intended to stop the next day but I didn't. I wrote 35 pages that day, much of it a complete re-working and I knew that evening I was going to do the whole book. There was no question that it was exciting to me and that I knew I was doing something good because, for no reason I could explain, the immovable blocks were beginning to join one another in a way I had never been able to make them do.

The word I have found for the experience was immersion. It is something

I intend to work to find again. Previously I had worked on the book and at the book but all at once I was immersed in the book. The book seemed to be carrying me instead of me pushing it. It was a very rare sensation. The book was much more real than anything else in my life then. As I went into the second week I had the sensation of being drawn very fine, as if I could thread myself through a needle. I seemed to have my own sense of the way things were while before I had always been listening over my shoulder to see if I could get a lead on the way things should go. I was out of life, under water, immersed.

I was, of course, making mistakes but they were my own mistakes and because of this they at least had the virtue of a certain consistency about them. I told no one what I was doing for fear of breaking the spell. Physically I must have shown it. In three and a half weeks' immersion I lost 20 pounds. One night my wife said "Bob, you seem so small" but the only physical effect I experienced was the phenomenon of the missing drinks. In the evening I would pour myself a drink and when I looked for it it would be empty. Evidently I was masking fatigue with alcohol and I must have drunk a great deal to sustain myself but I had no conscious desire to do this and never got drunk. At the end of 23 days I finished a manuscript which, when published, occupied 447 reasonably tightly printed pages. The following day, while walking down Madison Avenue, I collapsed in the street. It was, I tried to tell the doctor, a case of the bends, coming up too quick after my immersion, but he didn't understand.

What were the mistakes? I think I know most of them now. Most of them were the products of a lack of self-confidence caused by a lack of experience. Partially they were the results of waiting too long so that the assurance of youth, when one trusts one's judgement even if one has no reason to do so, gave way to the doubts of middle age, which is far more dangerous. I couldn't imagine who would be listening to me and who would want to read anything I wrote. As a consequence I determined to make them hear if I could. I overloaded scenes that were loaded enough as they were. If there was a legitimate chance to grab the reader by the lapels, I took it. I left nothing to trust and I presumed my potential reader was half deaf and half blind. I even worried about Marshall McLuhan and tried to make everything as visual as possible so I couldn't be accused of being a disciple of Gutenberg. The result is that there is too much muscle in the prose. I could see none of this then. When I turned in the book I thought it was thin and reedy and hollow and that wind could blow right through it. I now know that it is actually a rather dense book (in the best sense of that word), too dense, but I didn't know. Now perhaps I will.

Out of the whole experience I developed one tactic about writing that other writers might be able to profit from. I call it across the river and into the prose. During the Second World War a friend of mine serving in the Alaska Scouts noticed that when an American squad came to a river near the end of the day the squad would ford the river so they could build fires and dry their equipment and be dry when starting out in the morning. The squads with Indians always stopped on the near shore. The reason for this was another facet of immersion. In the morning the Americans, comfortable, warm and dry would tend to move very carefully and slowly across the tundra to avoid getting wet. They would detour for miles to avoid crossing a stream. The Indians on the other hand would start the day by fording the river and they didn't give a damn what happened to them after that. The worst had already been done.

I felt this could be applied to writing. There is a desire to finish a paragraph or chapter and enjoy the satisfaction of finishing. It is a good feeling. But in the morning there now is only that empty white blank sheet of paper to be filled. I have wasted days trying to regain a momentum I have lost. Now I don't allow myself the luxury of finishing, of getting dry and comfortable. When I am going good but have worked enough for the day I stop before finishing a paragraph I am anxious to finish and then I stop in the middle of a sentence. It is irritating and frustrating but also effective. There is nothing in writing harder to do than to start. But in the morning I finish the sentence that has been left unfinished and then I finish the paragraph and all at once I am in the river again.

Now I intend to write the book I intended to write all along, the one I used to think I had written, the one they would mention in the first paragraph of the obituary. There is a saying attributed to the French that no man should write his first novel until he is forty. This is the age when most Americans cease writing their last novels. I do hope the French are right.

Song

A breath of the mouth becomes a picture of the world . . . everything that man has ever thought and willed . . . depends on a moving breath of air.

Johann Herder

Pablo Neruda is Chile's most prominent poet. At the age of twenty Neruda published one of his most famous and enduring works, *Twenty Love Poems and A Desperate Song.* Since then, his dozens of volumes of poetry, essays, and memoirs have been translated into more than twenty-five languages. In the Latin American tradition of rewarding writers with diplomatic posts, Neruda spent much of his life as counselor official in Asia, the Far East, and Europe. After the Spanish Civil War, he joined the Communist Party and became a spokesperson for the Chilian left; at one time he was driven into exile where he wrote *General Song* (1950). Considered by many as his masterpiece, it contains 340 Whitmanesque poems, many with a Marxist political slant. "I have been convinced," he wrote, "that it is the poet's duty to take his stand along with the people." After a tumultuous life of commitment to both politics and poetry, he garnered worldwide recognition: The Stalin Prize for Literature, the Lenin Peace Prize, the first Honorary Doctor of Letters awarded by Oxford to a Latin American, and, in 1971, the Nobel Prize. After being nominated for President of Chile in 1970, he retired to spend his final years in a seaside home on Isla Negra near Valparaiso where he died in 1973.

"The Chilean Forest" and "The Word"

Pablo Neruda

Under the volcanoes, beside the snow-capped mountains, among the huge lakes, the fragrant, the silent, the tangled Chilean forest... My feet sink down into the dead leaves, a fragile twig crackles, the giant rauli trees rise in all their bristling height, a bird from the cold jungle passes over, flaps its wings, and stops in the sunless branches. And then, from its hideaway, it sings like an oboe... The wild scent of the laurel, the dark scent of the boldo herb, enter my nostrils and flood my whole being... The cypress of the Guaitecas blocks my way... This is a vertical world: a nation of birds, a plenitude of leaves... I stumble over a rock, dig up the uncovered hollow, an enormous spider covered with red hairs stares up at me, motionless, as huge as a crab... A golden carabus beetle blows its mephitic breath at me, as its brilliant rainbow disappears like lightning... Going on, I pass through a forest of ferns much taller than I am: from their cold green eyes sixty tears splash down on my face and, behind me, their fans go on quivering for a long time... A decaying tree trunk: what a treasure!... Black and blue mushrooms have given it ears, red parasite plants have covered it with rubies, other lazy plants have let it borrow their beards, and a snake springs out of the rotted body like a sudden breath, as if the spirit of the dead trunk were

Source: "The Chilean Forest" and "The Word" from Memoirs, translated from the Spanish by Hardie St. Martin. Confieso que he vivido: Memoirs. Copyright © the estate of Pablo Neruda, 1974. Translation copyright © Farrar, Straus, and Giroux, Inc., 1976, 1977.

slipping away from it... Farther along, each tree stands away from its fellows... They soar up over the carpet of the secretive forest, and the foliage of each has its own style, linear, bristling, ramulose, lanceolate, as if cut by shears moving in infinite ways... A gorge; below, the crystal water slides over granite and jasper... A butterfly goes past, bright as a lemon, dancing between the water and the sunlight... Close by, innumerable calceolarias nod their little yellow heads in greeting... High up, red copihues (*Lapageria rosea*) dangle like drops from the magic forest's arteries... The red copihue is the blood flower, the white copihue is the snow flower... A fox cuts through the silence like a flash, sending a shiver through the leaves, but silence is the law of the plant kingdom... The barely audible cry of some bewildered animal far off... The piercing interruption of a hidden bird... The vegetable world keeps up its low rustle until a storm churns up all the music of the earth.

Anyone who hasn't been in the Chilean forest doesn't know this planet.

I have come out of that landscape, that mud, that silence, to roam, to go singing through the world.

... You can say anything you want, yessir, but it's the words that sing, they soar and descend... I bow to them... I love them, I cling to them, I run them down, I bite into them, I melt them down... I love words so much... The unexpected ones... The ones I wait for greedily or stalk until, suddenly, they drop... Vowels I love... They glitter like colored stones, they leap like silver fish, they are foam, thread, metal, dew... I run after certain words... They are so beautiful that I want to fit them all into my poems... I catch them in midflight, as they buzz past, I trap them, clean them, peel them, I set myself in front of the dish, they have a crystalline texture to me, vibrant, ivory, vegetable, oily, like fruit, like algae, like agates, like olives... And then I stir them, I shake them, I drink them, I gulp them down, I mash them, I garnish them, I let them go... I leave them in my poem like stalactites, like slivers of polished wood, like coals, pickings from a shipwreck, gifts from the waves... Everything exists in the word... An idea goes through a complete change because one word shifted its place, or because another settled down like a spoiled little thing inside a phrase that was not expecting her but obeys her... They have shadow, transparence, weight, feathers, hair, and everything they gathered from so much rolling down the river, from so much wandering from country to country, from being roots so long... They are very ancient and very new... They live in the bier, hidden away, and in the budding flower... What a great language I have, it's a fine language we inherited from the fierce conquistadors... They strode over the giant cordilleras, over the rugged Americas, hunting for potatoes, sausages, beans, black tobacco, gold, corn, fried eggs, with a voracious appetite not found in the world since then . . . They swallowed up everything, religions, pyramids, tribes, idolatries just like the ones they brought along in their huge sacks . . . Wherever they went, they razed the land . . . But words fell like pebbles out of the boots of the barbarians, out of their beards, their helmets, their horseshoes, luminous words that were left glittering here . . . our language. We came up losers . . . We came up winners . . . They carried off the gold and left us the gold . . . They carried everything off and left us everything . . . They left us the words.

Stanley Kunitz published his first collection of poems, *Intellectual Things,* after graduating from Harvard. He has since produced four more volumes of poetry, including *The Testing-Tree* (1971) and a widely acclaimed translation, *Poems of Akhmatova* (1973). The Brandeis Medal of Achievement, awarded in 1965, cited his poetry as "combining a classical strength of language and vision." Kunitz remarks that "I keep reading the masters, because they infect me with human possibility." In the past decade he has served as editor of the Yale Series of Younger Poets and Consultant in Poetry to the Library of Congress. In 1974 he was elected to the American Academy of Arts and Letters. *Selected Poems* won the Pulitzer Prize in 1958, while his most recent work, *The Poems of Stanley Kunitz 1928–1978,* won the Lenore Marshall Poetry Prize in 1980.

Swimming in Lake Chauggogagogmanchaug-gagogchabunagungamaugg

Pre-memory floods the mind
like molten lava on the sands.
—Anna Akhmatova

Stanley Kunitz

When I was a boy in Massachusetts one of my favorite haunts was Lake Webster, named from the town of its location. It was a lovely lake, in a then relatively unspoiled countryside, but no lovelier, I suppose, than several other lakes and ponds that I could have frequented nearer my home in Worcester. The reason for my preference was that I had made a thrilling discovery while browsing among the books of local history in the Worcester Public Library. There I learned that the Indians who once lived on the shores of Lake Webster had a word of their own for it: *Chauggogagogmanchauggagog-chabunagungamaugg*. To think that this was reputed to be the longest lake-name in the world! To know, moreover, that this fantastic porridge of syllables made sense, and what delicious sense, signifying: "I-fish-on-my-side, you-fish-on-your-side, nobody-fishes-in-the-middle!" I practiced how to say it, priding myself on talking Indian . . . nor to this very day have I forgotten the combination.

Source: Copyright © 1966 by Stanley Kunitz. By permission of Little, Brown and Company in association with the Atlantic Monthly Press.

To utter that mouthful, to give the lake its secret name, was somehow to possess it, to assert my power over the spot, as by an act of magic. Years later, when I became interested in philology, I read, with a sense of *déjà vu*, the theory that in the beginning of the human adventure a word consisted of a long and elaborate sound or series of sounds associated with the ritual of the tribe and expressed in a chant with appropriate gestures; that into each word-sentence, as in extant primitive languages, a whole complex of thought, emotion and feeling was packed.

One of the familiar grievances of the modern poet is that language gets more and more shabby and debased in everyday usage, until even the great words that men must live by lose their lustre. How to make words potent and magical again, how to restore their lost vitality? A poet is a man who yearns to swim in Lake Chauggogagogmanchauggagogchabunagungamaugg, not in Lake Webster. He loves a language that reaches all the way back to its primitive condition. So it is that the words of a poem are full of subterranean electric feelings, pent-up music, sleeping gestures. A poem trembles on the verge of lapsing into music, of breaking into dance: but its virtue lies in resisting the temptation—in remaining language. There is an ideal lyric in my head whose words flow together to form a single word-sentence, an unremitting stream of sound, as in the Indian lake-name; I am not reconciled to the knowledge that I shall never be able to write it.

A good deal of craft goes into the making of a poem, much more than most readers and some writers suspect. Poems are not produced by the will; and craft alone, though it may assure the manufacture of a reasonably competent set of verses, is insufficient for the creation of a poem. How many times have I heard my poet-friends, in the doldrums between poems, despair of the possibility of writing another! Solitude and a fierce attentiveness precede insight, which other ages could call "vision" without embarrassment. "The man wipes his breath from the window pane," wrote Yeats, "and laughs in his delight at all the varied scene." Or as Blake phrased it earlier: "If the doors of perception were cleansed, everything would appear to man as it is, infinite."

The poets whom I most admire look on life with a watchful and affectionate eye, unfogged by sentimentality. They study the things of the world, but not from the world's view. One of their disciplines is to resist the temptation to skim poems off the top of their minds. Poets need stamina as much as they need imagination. Indeed, when we speak of the imagination, we imply an activity of surplus energy . . . energy beyond what is required for mere survival. An interviewer once asked me a rather brash question: "What do you consider to be your chief asset as a poet?"—to which I gave the reply that I thought he deserved: "My ability to stay awake after midnight." Perhaps I was more serious than I intended. Certainly the poems of mine that I am most committed to are those that I recall fighting for hardest, through the anxious hours, until I managed to come out on the other side of fatigue, where I could begin to breathe again, as though the air had changed and I had found my second wind.

One such poem that I can offer, not without trepidation, for comment is "End of Summer":*

> *An agitation of the air*
> *A perturbation of the light*
> *Admonished me the unloved year*
> *Would turn on its hinge that night.*
>
> *I stood in the disenchanted field*
> *Amid the stubble and the stones,*
> *Amazed, while a small worm lisped to me*
> *The song of my marrow-bones.*
>
> *Blue poured into summer blue,*
> *A hawk broke from his cloudless tower,*
> *The roof of the silo blazed, and I knew*
> *That part of my life was over.*
>
> *Already the iron door of the north*
> *Clangs open: birds, leaves, snows*
> *Order their populations forth,*
> *And a cruel wind blows.*

I can remember how and where that poem began more than a decade ago. It was an afternoon in late September. I was chopping weeds in the field behind my house in Bucks County, Pennsylvania. Toward sunset I heard a commotion in the sky and looked up, startled to observe wedge after wedge of wild geese honking downriver, with their long necks pointing south. I watched until the sun sank and the air turned chill. Then I put away my garden tools and walked back to the house, shivering with a curious premonition. After dinner I went upstairs to my study and tried until dawn to get the words down on paper. Nothing came that seemed right to me. Five days later I had hundreds of lines, but they still added up to nothing. In the middle of the fifth night I experienced a revelation: what was wrong with my enterprise was that I was attempting to compose a descriptive piece about the migration

---

*From *The Poems of Stanley Kunitz 1928–1978*. Copyright 1953 by Stanley Kunitz. By permission of Little, Brown & Co., in association with the Atlantic Monthly Press.

of the birds, whereas it was the disturbance of the heart that really concerned me and that insisted on a language. At this point I opened the window, as it were, and let the geese fly out. Then the poem came with a rush.

In my first draft the opening lines read:

> *The agitation of the air,*
> *The perturbation of the light....*

I write my poems by speaking them—they are meant to be heard. What I heard displeased my ear because the plethora of "the's" made too thick a sound. The indefinite articles that I introduced in my revision serve to open up the lines and to accelerate the tempo.

In the second stanza the words that interest me most are "amazed" and "lisped." Both of them were afterthoughts. Originally my posture was "surprised," while the invertebrate redundantly "sang" its song. "Amazed" is much more open-mouthed and suspended than "surprised"; moreover, it hooks on to "admonished" and "amid" before it, to "marrow" in the next line, and to "blazed" in the next stanza. At the same time it relieves the passage of a frightful excess of sibilants. As for "lisped," I consider it the perfectly right and proper thing for a small worm to do.

The image of the roof of the silo flashing back the sunlight suggests an epiphany to me, the precise moment of illumination. Actually, I had no silo on my place in the Delaware Valley: it forced itself into my poem, to erupt as the climax of a progression, out of another landscape that had once been dear to me, and I recognized instantaneously that it came with the imprimatur of psychological truth.

In the final stanza the opening of "the iron door of the north" releases the arctic blast before which, in sequence, are driven "birds, leaves, snows," three variants of migration. After the fact I am aware that here the sounds become harsher, as the rhythm is sprung and the strong stressing hammered out. In my own reading of the poem I give the concluding syllable an almost painful protraction, as though the wind would never stop blowing.

Earlier I said that I had let the geese fly out of the poem. Was I mistaken? It occurs to me now that their ghosts are present, their wings keep beating, from the first word to the last in "End of Summer."

William Heyen holds degrees from the State University of New York at Brockport and Ohio University. He has published in more than 100 periodicals including *The New Yorker, Harper's, Southern Review,* and *Poetry* magazine which in 1978 awarded him the Eunize Tietjens Memorial Prize for poetry. In addition to a Guggenheim Fellowship, he has served as a Fulbright lecturer to Germany out of which grew his most controversial collection, *The Swastika Poems* (1977). His most recent work includes *Long Island Light: Poems and a Memoir* (1979) and *Lord Dragonfly: Five Sequences* (1981).

Fishing the Poem

William Heyen

The world does not burst in upon the [poet]. He waits, riding the boat of the unconscious, for a sign.

THE RETURN

"I will touch things and things and no more thoughts."

Robinson Jeffers

My boat slowed on the still water,
stopped in a thatch of lilies.
The moon leaned over the white lilies.

I waited for a sign, and stared
at the hooded water. On the far shore
brush broke, a deer broke cover.

I waited for a sign, and waited.
The moon lit the lilies to candles.
Their light reached down the water

Source: Adapted from "What Do The Trees Say," by William Heyen, American Poets in 1976, edited by William Heyen, Copyright © 1976, Bobbs-Merrill Co., 1976.

to a dark flame, a fish: it hovered
under the pads, the pond held it
in its dim depths as though in amber.

Green, still, balanced in its own life,
breathing small breaths of light, this
was the world's oldest wonder, the arrow

of thought, the branch that all words
break against, the deep fire, the pure poise
of an object, the pond's presence, the pike.

"The world's oldest wonder" was "the world's single wonder" in draft, so strongly do I feel about the necessity of staring—it is harder, now that I am getting older, to *see*—, so much do I want to eschew talk and make a language that images and deepens the world as precisely as language can, so convinced am I that the best poems from "Sir Patrick Spens" to Ginsberg's "Sunflower Sutra" to Archibald MacLeish's "Companions" begin with the gold combs and battered crowns and evening grasses our senses must always know. Jeffers once told an aspirer that the young man had enough soul in his poems and needed *body*. "The Return" does not freeze that fish by naming it, does not for long explain the world, does not end the waiting and searching for signs any more than one of my oak poems does. But I am glad that the pike rose to me as I fished that poem.

Technique

I have always regarded technique as a means, not an end in itself. One must, of course, master technique; at the same time, one must not become enslaved by it. One must understand that the purpose of technique is to transmit the inner meaning, the message, of the music.

Pablo Casals

Marvin Bell studied poetry at the State University of Iowa Writer's Workshop where he now teaches. He has received the Lamont Poetry Award, the Bess Hopkin Award from *Poetry* magazine, and the Emily Clark Balch Prize from *The Virginia Quarterly Review*. *Stars Which See, Stars Which Do Not See* was a 1977 finalist for the National Book Award. A prolific writer, Bell has stated that he believes his writing was only an apprenticeship until age 40. He has held Guggenheim and National Endowment for the Arts Fellowship, taught at the Bread Loaf Writers' Conference, and written an off-and-on column of informal essays for *American Poetry Review* from which "The Technique of the Right Attitude" is excerpted. An expanded version will appear in a forthcoming collection of Bell's prose to be published by the University of Michigan Poets on Poetry Series.

The Technique of the Right Attitude

Marvin Bell

I propose to describe (in the sense of "talk 'round") a poetry of consciousness, economy and profound ease. In so doing, I will be talking about mental disciplines which require time and effort and on which everything else in the writing of poetry may depend.

I take for epigraph two short texts. The first is by Charlie Mingus, the jazz bassist, speaking about creativity in the July, 1977 issue of *Mainliner*:

> *Love of something sparks creativity. . . . You get hooked on something early and that's your outlet. When I was a baby, I heard some tune on my mother's crystal set—da-da-da-da-da—I was paralyzed. After that, always when I was unhappy, when I got a whipping, I went to the piano. And it all came out. First the piano. Later the bass.*
>
> *That's once I got hooked. The other time was when I first heard Charlie Parker. I was a studio musician then, but hearing Bird changed my life. Charlie Parker was the essence of creativity. Bird wasn't just playing, he was composing as he played. And where did it come from? Where in Kansas City did he learn to quote Stravinsky while he was playing?*
>
> *Creativity is more than just being different. Being different isn't necessarily being original. Anybody can play weird; that's easy. What's hard is to be as*

simple as Bach. What you have to do is know where you're coming from, be able to do what's gone before, but go on from there in your own way . . .

My son's a painter. All through school his teachers tell him he's a genius. I tell him to paint me an apple that looks like an apple before he paints me one that doesn't. Go where you go, but start from somewhere recognizable. Making the simple complicated is commonplace; making the complicated simple, awesomely simple, that's creativity.

The second of the texts I propose for its epigraphic value is by Samuel Johnson, from his *Preface to Shakespeare*. James Wright, in speaking about his own poetic values, incorporated this Johnson statement into his own remarks in the 1966 anthology, *The Distinctive Voice*, edited by William J. Martz. This is Johnson:

Nothing can please many or please long but just representations of general nature. Particular manners can be known to few, and few only can judge how nearly they are copied. The irregular combinations of fanciful invention may delight awhile, by that novelty of which the common satiety of life sends us all in quest. But the pleasures of sudden wonder are soon exhausted, and the mind can only repose on the stability of truth.

Johnson equates truth in art with "just representations of general nature." Back of such an equation rests the concept of recognition. "Particular manners can be known to few, and few only can judge how nearly they are copied."

In keeping with the Johnson text, therefore, my intention is to tell you only things that you already know. For example, we know what most people think of poetry. Most people do not recognize just representations of their general natures in poetry at all. Most people think poetry is lies and decoration, mystification and good manners. It seems too strenuous, too strident, at other times too frivolous, to be read without a feeling afterwards of diminishment. Or it poses: the poet as melancholic sensitive, the poet as the wounded, the poet as the self-righteous, writing as Literature. Most people know what poetry is. Poetry is a waste of time.

Therefore, when poets show up in popular art, they show up as clowns or dopes. Perhaps you remember the poet of the old television series called "Meet Millie." His name, alas, was Marvin, and his odes to bathtubs and the like destroyed any interest I might have had in serious poetry at the time. In the re-runs of Ernie Kovacs, you can see his poet, Percy Dovetonsils, endlessly cooing "Flower in the Crannied Wall." And there's Henry Gibson, with his oversized daisy and his not-quite-funny verses. Even "Happy Days," the current television hit series, once offered us a young Bohemian lady marvelling over that wonderful book of poems, *Warts on My Soul*.

Of course, it isn't poetry that is so widely jeered and dismissed. It's poeticizing. "Poeticizing" is what I would call it. A good copy desk editor would probably call it, simply, "overwriting." Unfortunately, the word "poetry" is common, while the word "poeticizing" is rare. In the common vernacular, "poetry" and "poeticizing" mean the same thing. "Oh, that's only poetry," is what people say. Therefore, I must agree with those who not only say about poetry, "I, too, dislike it," but with those who actually do. What I dislike in poems, and what I think defeats them, is the *poitry* in them, the thoughtless stylization that becomes the style of the art of one's time, what my friend Stanley Plumly calls "creative writing." (The other thing I think defeats poems is the prose in them, but that's another matter.)

Now obviously, I couldn't be offering these remarks if I didn't, like you, carry a sense, if not a definition, of good poetry, and if I didn't love it and learn from it. Nonetheless, I think it may be helpful to remind ourselves occasionally that language is rarely the vehicle for truth and beauty. One need only read the newspapers and magazines, listen to television or radio, or—alas—read most poems to know that language is, most of the time, the vehicle for lies, distortions, hyperbole and just plain busywork.

It is my hypothesis that, in poetry, such errors can derive from the strain of aesthetic ambition: from thinking of poetry as universal art rather than as personal expression and from thinking of poetry as righteous vision rather than as obsessive viewpoints.

We know that poetry begins in self-expression and/or in verbal game-playing. Verbal game-playing is what Auden was endorsing when he said that he saw no promise in the student who wished to write poems because he or she had things to say, but did see promise in the student who wanted to hang around words to see what *they* had to say. If self-expression by itself leads to what we might call "popular poetry," distinguished by its sentimentality, verbal gamesmanship by itself leads to what we might call "literary poetry," distinguished by its on-high presumptions and its reductiveness, whether in the Academy or in the streets. It is my opinion now that neither self-expression nor gamesmanship are sufficient apprenticeships or happy pursuits unless they are combined with mental attitudes which have little to do with verse forms or syntax, or with what is on our minds.

William Stafford is a good example of a poet who plays the game of poetry, though not at all as Auden would have it played. He writes all the time and, like all of our best poets, he is willing to fail. In a short essay about his method, called "A Way of Writing," . . . he takes the position that words are cheap. "A writer," says Stafford, "is not so much someone who has something to say as he is someone who has found a process that will bring about new things he would not have thought of if he had not started to say them."

Stafford is easy about the materials of poetry. He trusts them. He is able to use anything that occurs to him because he unburdens himself of the weight of significance. He doesn't have to play for keeps. It is sometimes, he says, like practice. In this respect, I have noticed, as I'm certain that many of you have, how often the poem written as an exercise, perhaps on assignment, turns out better than the poem which was written out of great ambition for our perceptions.

Yet perception is, in the end, the better part of poetry: that stability of truth on which the mind can find, according to Samuel Johnson, its only repose. Perception has two meanings: sight and insight. I believe that both sight and insight derive from fierce consciousness, whether it begins in looking at a small object or in paying attention to all of the implications and resonances of an idea or image. "Paint me an apple that looks like an apple before you paint me one that doesn't." I believe, also, that conscious perception is our only path to both the conscious world and the unconscious. Everyone knows that Frost's poem, "Stopping by Woods on a Snowy Evening" is about taking a breather between towns. And everyone knows what it's *really* about.

I mean to emphasize here a sense of consciousness as awareness. P. D. Ouspensky's first five lectures, available in *The Psychology of Man's Possible Evolution,* will serve to elaborate on this.

There, he refuses the usual distinction between the conscious and the unconscious. Instead, he defines four states of consciousness: sleep, waking state (in which we are influenced by the dreams and slight sensory impressions of sleep, and which differs little from sleep), self-consciousness (not the nervousness of the adolescent but adult consciousness of the self) and objective consciousness.

It is Ouspensky's view that, although man has the possibility of these four states of consciousness, he actually lives in only two states. One part passes in sleep, and the other part in what is called "waking state," though in reality his waking state differs very little from sleep.

"In ordinary life," he says, "man knows nothing of 'objective consciousness'" (the fourth state). The third state, "self-consciousness," occurs but rarely and sometimes goes unrecognized. According to Ouspensky, "... these glimpses of consciousness come in exceptional moments, in highly emotional states, in moments of danger, in very new and unexpected circumstances and situations; or sometimes in quite ordinary moments when nothing in particular happens." Ouspensky further claims that what we remember long after—say, from childhood—we remember because those were our conscious (that is, self-conscious) moments: our moments of heightened awareness, if you like.

Now suppose we were able to banish from the final versions of our poem all lies disguised as the truth, including distortions and exaggerations, all hypotheses about which we know better, and all the arty overwriting. What would be left, in fact, would be perception in both senses of the word. Sight would occur as telling detail, and insight as wholly inevitable suggestion and idea.

I have been describing an attitude here. I mean to suggest that one's writing benefits from a certain mental position and emotion toward the world and the poem: a heightened awareness at the least and a fierce consciousness at best, along with an easy feeling about what a poem is. About that *easy* feeling—you know, were you to keep always in mind models of good poems, you could never write a poem unlike your models. Self-expression, acceptance, paying attention, sticking to the subject (that is, using and developing rather than mentioning and accumulating), getting the facts straight: these don't sound like very high falutin' aesthetic principles. That's why I like 'em.

Moreover, such simple principles can help us, I think, to approach what Ouspensky calls "objective consciousness," and an emphasis upon unself-conscious awareness leads us to the mystery and richness of life. In this regard, I am going to incorporate here a lovely, inspiring essay by the late Soetsu Yanagi. Dr. Yanagi, who was Director of the Museum of Folk-Crafts in Tokyo, delivered this essay during his visit in 1952 to the Archie Bray Foundation in Helena, Montana. It concerns a kind of pilgrimage Dr. Yanagi made from Japan to Korea, and I must ask you to remember that the rural Korea he describes may no longer exist. The essay is titled, "Mystery of Beauty."

> In South Korea stands the village Ampo, a lonely hamlet, remote from towns. To visit this village was a hope I had long cherished, for I had seen many examples of beautiful turnery (wood turning) made by the villagers. Nearly all Korean woodwork, especially turnery, suffers some deformity in its shape. But this slight crookedness always gives us a certain peculiar asymmetrical beauty, an indescribable charm that entices us into a sense of beauty that is free and unrestricted. From what source and by what means Korean craftsmen obtain such natural asymmetrical beauty had long been a question for me.
>
> In Japan we find also a great deal of turned works. Some are extremely good, made so precisely that they are almost perfect in shape. But their symmetrical perfection lacks the quality of unrestricted beauty. In turning there is an accepted rule that the wood used should be thoroughly dried; otherwise cracks will almost certainly appear. In Japan the wood is air dried for at least two or three years. This is common sense. In modern factories, of course, the drying is done quickly in kilns. In any case, all turnery should be produced from well dried wood.
>
> Fortunately, I was favored with a rare visit to that Korean village where those beautiful turned goods are made. I was excited by the opportunity of seeing these Korean craftsmen at work because I thought that I might grasp the mysterious beauty of their products.
>
> When I arrived after a long, hard trip, I noticed at once beside their work-

shops many big blocks of pine ready to be lathed. To my great astonishment all of them were sap green and by no means ready for use. Imagine my surprise when a workman set one of these blocks in a lathe and began to turn it. The pine was so green that turning it produced a spray redolent of the scent of resin. This use of green wood perplexed me greatly, for it defies a basic rule of turnery. I asked the artisan, 'Why do you use such green wood? Cracks will appear pretty soon.' 'What does it matter?' was the calm answer. I was amazed by this Zen-monk-like response. I felt sweat on my forehead. Yet I dared to ask him, 'How can we use something that leaks?' 'Just mend it' was his simple answer.

I was amazed to discover that these artisans mend their turnery so artistically and ingeniously that a cracked piece seems better than a perfect one. Consequently they do not care whether it is cracked or not. Our common sense is of no use to Koreans at all. They live in a world of 'thusness,' not of 'must or must not.' Their way of making things is so natural that man-made rules are meaningless to them. They are attached neither to the perfect piece nor to the imperfect. So it was that at this moment when I received the artisan's unexpected answer I came to understand for the first time the mystery of the asymmetrical nature of Korean turnery. Because Korean artisans use green wood, their wares inevitably deform while drying. Therefore, the asymmetry is but a natural outcome of their state of mind, not the result of conscious choice. In short, their minds are free from any attachment to symmetry or asymmetry. The deformity of their work is the result of nonchalance, freedom from restriction. This explains why Japanese turnery looks hard and cold in comparison with Korean. We are attached to perfection; we want to make the perfect piece. But what is human perfection after all?

In modern art, as everyone knows, the beauty of deformity is very often emphasized, insisted upon. But how different is Korean deformity. The former is produced deliberately, the latter naturally. Korean work is merely the natural result of the artisan's state of mind, which is free from dualistic man-made rules. He makes his asymmetrical turnery not because he regards the asymmetrical form beautiful or the symmetrical ugly but because, as he works, he is perfectly unaware of such polarities. He is quite free from conflict between the beautiful and the ugly. Here lies buried the mystery of the endless beauty of the Korean artisan's work. He simply makes what he makes without pretension.

One who has had the chance to visit a Korean potter's shed may notice that the wheel used for throwing pots is never exactly true. Sometimes it is so crudely mounted that it is not even horizontal. The asymmetrical nature of Korean pots results in part, therefore, from the uneven movement of the wheel. But we must understand that Koreans do not make such wheels because they like unevenness and dislike evenness. Rather they simply construct their wheels in a happy-go-lucky way. This unevenness, then, is but a natural outcome of the untrammeled state of their minds. They live just as circumstances permit, without any conception of artificiality. Of course, if the wheel is canted too much, they may correct it to some extent, but even then it will not be precise. They are scarcely troubled by accuracy or inaccuracy, for in their world these qualities are not yet differentiated. This state of mind is the source from which flows the beauty of Korean pots.

Why did our tea-masters, men of keen eyes, prefer Korean pots to all others? The asymmetrical beauty, free from all pretention, was immensely attractive to their aesthetic eyes. They so ardently loved to gaze upon those Korean pots that they finally tried to analyze the beauty expressed in them. They enumerated ten virtues as the elements of which their beauty consisted. It is quite remarkable that the eyes of our tea-masters penetrated so deeply into the beauty of these pots.

Paradoxically, however, their very analysis initiated the history of an erroneous attitude which has poisoned nearly all the latter tea-potters in Japan. They imagined that they could make good pots by isolating the indispensable elements of beauty which characterized Korean tea utensils. But what was the result? In spite of their careful craftsmanship and passionate love of beauty, their analytical self-consciousness has never been able to produce pots as beautiful as the original Korean ware. Why? The reason is obvious: they did not understand that the Korean pots were not the result of intellectual analysis but of a natural and spontaneous condition of the mind. If our tea-masters had told the Korean potters about the ten virtues, the Koreans would not have known what to say.

The Koreans simply made pots, while the Japanese proceeded from thought to action. We have made nice things, but they are different. We proceed upon a conscious differentiation of the beautiful and the ugly, while the Korean's work is done before such differentiation takes place. Which is better? I do not say that the analytical approach is useless, but if we are confined by analysis, we cannot be assured of producing pots of indescribable beauty. Why is it that self-conscious potters cannot make beautiful pots with ease? Because it is extremely hard for them to make things in that state of mind described by Buddhists as 'thusness.'

All beautiful crafts are nothing more than the expression of attained Buddhahood. Enlightenment means liberation from all duality. If we want to make a truly beautiful object, we must before all else reach this state of mind which is free. In comparison to this radical condition, degree of skill, depth of knowledge, even the quality of materials are secondary considerations. This is the utter simple truth implicit in every Santo or Retablo painted by those Mexican devotees of the humble mind.

Of course it is far better to have good training, knowledge, and well chosen materials, but the one absolutely indispensable thing is the attainment of that state of mind which is free from all dualistic fetters. If this one condition is lacking, all skill, knowledge and materials will be wasted.

Should we not include in the category of "dualistic fetters" that of form and content? And should we not also include influence and originality or, if you prefer, "tradition and the individual talent"? For poetry remains personal expression. In one's own language. Not trying to sound like others. Not trying not to.

And style takes care of itself. Eventually, we all come to say things in our own way. Elegant diction, rhyme and meter are not more expressive or precise than other ways, but are merely signs of a style. Nor do colloquial diction, continually varying rhythms and an absence of rhyme signify a greater sincerity, but again merely a style.

And since I don't want to waste your time, I'll tell you right now the secrets of writing poetry. Since all gall is divided into three parts, there are three of them. First, one learns to write by reading (of course one has to be writing too). That is, the quality of what one reads makes a difference, and the quality of one's reading attention makes a difference. That's number one.

Number two (and not everyone may agree with this), I believe that language, compared to the materials of other art forms, has only one thing going for it: the ability to be precise. All suggestion in a poem, and the quality of the emotion in a poem, derive from precision. All other so-called "aspects" of poetry—even to rhythm and sound—are in its service. Actually, words cannot be precise about *things*. No matter how particular the description of a *thing* in a poem, when the poem moves on the description of the thing remains limited and the thing described remains one of a class, not one of a kind. What words *can* be precise about is ideas, ideas that come from the relationships of the modestly particular things in a poem. The things, in turn, derive from the workings of sensibility, which derives from personal obsessions. Therefore, serious poetry is profoundly adult. It is an adult art, deriving its finest moments from a fully developed heart and mind. Trusting oneself to the language as Stafford does—"adventuring in the language," as he phrases it—implies the richness of the mature self behind that trust. Therefore, the second "secret" is to look into the distance—not only to see how small one is, but also to see how far one can go.

And the third and most important secret is that, if you do anything seriously for a long time, you get better at it.

Flannery O'Connor studied at the State University of Iowa Writer's Workshop with Paul Engle. She spent most of her short life suffering from an hereditary disease and living at home in rural Georgia raising peacocks. Although she published two novels, she is best known for *A Good Man Is Hard to Find* (1955) and *Everything that Rises Must Converge* (1965), both collections of stories that include works now considered among America's classic pieces of short fiction. Before her death in 1964, she won a National Institute of Arts and Letters Grant and a First Prize in the O'Henry Awards. A second O'Henry Award was granted posthumously in 1965. Her letters, collected by Sally Fitzgerald in *A Habit of Being* (1979), reveal her to have been a woman of remarkable optimism and courage. "I have to write to discover what I am doing," she noted. "Like the old lady, I don't know so well what I think until I see what I say; then I have to say it over again." The following essay was first delivered to a writers' conference held at a southern college for women.

Writing Short Stories

Flannery O'Connor

I have heard people say that the short story was one of the most difficult literary forms, and I've always tried to decide why people feel this way about what seems to me to be one of the most natural and fundamental ways of human expression. After all, you begin to hear and tell stories when you're a child, and there doesn't seem to be anything very complicated about it. I suspect that most of you have been telling stories all your lives, and yet here you sit—come to find out how to do it.

Then last week, after I had written down some of these serene thoughts to use here today, my calm was shattered when I was sent seven of your manuscripts to read.

After this experience, I found myself ready to admit, if not that the short story is one of the most difficult literary forms, at least that it is more difficult for some than for others.

I still suspect that most people start out with some kind of ability to tell a story but that it gets lost along the way. Of course, the ability to create life with words is essentially a gift. If you have it in the first place, you can develop it; if you don't have it, you might as well forget it.

But I have found that the people who don't have it are frequently the ones hell-bent on writing stories. I'm sure anyway that they are the ones who write the books and the magazine articles on how-to-write-short-stories. I have a friend who is taking a correspondence course in this subject, and she has passed a few of the chapter headings on to me—such as, "The Story Formula for Writers," "How to Create Characters," "Let's Plot!" This form of corruption is costing her twenty-seven dollars.

I feel that discussing story-writing in terms of plot, character, and theme is like trying to describe the expression on a face by saying where the eyes, nose, and mouth are. I've heard students say, "I'm very good with plot, but I can't do a thing with character," or, "I have this theme but I don't have a plot for it," and once I heard one say, "I've got the story but I don't have any technique."

Technique is a word they all trot out. I talked to a writers' club once, and during the question time, one good soul said, "Will you give me the technique for the frame-within-a-frame short story?" I had to admit I was so ignorant I didn't even know what that was, but she assured me there was such a thing because she had entered a contest to write one and the prize was fifty dollars.

But setting aside the people who have no talent for it, there are others who do have the talent but who flounder around because they don't really know what a story is.

I suppose that obvious things are the hardest to define. Everybody thinks he knows what a story is. But if you ask a beginning student to write a story, you're liable to get almost anything—a reminiscence, an episode, an opinion, an anecdote, anything under the sun but a story. A story is a complete dramatic action—and in good stories, the characters are shown through the action and the action is controlled through the characters, and the result of this is meaning that derives from the whole presented experience. I myself prefer to say that a story is a dramatic event that involves a person because he is a person, and a particular person—that is, because he shares in the general human condition and in some specific human situation. A story always involves, in a dramatic way, the mystery of personality. I lent some stories to a country lady who lives down the road from me, and when she returned them, she said, "Well, them stories just gone and shown you how some folks *would* do," and I thought to myself that that was right; when you write stories, you have to be content to start exactly there—showing how some specific folks *will* do, *will* do in spite of everything.

Now this is a very humble level to have to begin on, and most people who think they want to write stories are not willing to start there. They want to write about problems, not people; or about abstract issues, not concrete situations. They have an idea, or a feeling, or an overflowing ego, or they want to Be A Writer, or they want to give their wisdom to the world in a simple-enough way for the world to be able to absorb it. In any case, they don't have a story and they wouldn't be willing to write it if they did; and in the absence of a story, they set out to find a theory or a formula or a technique.

Now none of this is to say that when you write a story, you are supposed to forget or give up any moral position that you hold. Your beliefs will be the light by which you see, but they will not be what you see and they will not be a substitute for seeing. For the writer of fiction, everything has its testing point in the eye, and the eye is an organ that eventually involves the whole personality, and as much of the world as can be got into it. It involves judgment. Judgment is something that begins in the act of vision, and when it does not, or when it becomes separated from vision, then a confusion exists in the mind which transfers itself to the story.

Fiction operates through the senses, and I think one reason that people find it so difficult to write stories is that they forget how much time and patience is required to convince through the senses. No reader who doesn't actually experience, who isn't made to feel, the story is going to believe anything the fiction writer merely tells him. The first and most obvious characteristic of fiction is that it deals with reality through what can be seen, heard, smelt, tasted, and touched.

Now this is something that can't be learned only in the head; it has to be learned in the habits. It has to become a way that you habitually look at things. The fiction writer has to realize that he can't create compassion with compassion, or emotion with emotion, or thought with thought. He has to provide all these things with a body; he has to create a world with weight and extension.

I have found that the stories of beginning writers usually bristle with emotion, but *whose* emotion is often very hard to determine. Dialogue frequently proceeds without the assistance of any characters that you can actually see, and uncontained thought leaks out of every corner of the story. The reason is usually that the student is wholly interested in his thoughts and his emotions and not in his dramatic action, and that he is too lazy or highfalutin to descend to the concrete where fiction operates. He thinks that judgment exists in one place and sense-impression in another. But for the fiction writer, judgment begins in the details he sees and how he sees them.

Fiction writers who are not concerned with these concrete details are guilty of what Henry James called "weak specification." The eye will glide over their words while the attention goes to sleep. Ford Madox Ford taught that you couldn't have a man appear long enough to sell a newspaper in a story unless you put him there with enough detail to make the reader see him.

I have a friend who is taking acting classes in New York from a Russian lady who is supposed to be very good at teaching actors. My friend wrote me that the first month they didn't speak a line, they only learned to see. Now learning to see is the basis for learning all the arts except music. I know a good many fiction writers who paint, not because they're any good at painting, but because it helps their writing. It forces them to look at things. Fiction writing is very seldom a matter of saying things; it is a matter of showing things.

However, to say that fiction proceeds by the use of detail does not mean the simple, mechanical piling-up of detail. Detail has to be controlled by some overall purpose, and every detail has to be put to work for you. Art is selective. What is there is essential and creates movement.

Now all this requires time. A good short story should not have less meaning than a novel, nor should its action be less complete. Nothing essential to the main experience can be left out of a short story. All the action has to be satisfactorily accounted for in terms of motivation, and there has to be a beginning, a middle, and an end, though not necessarily in that order. I think many people decide that they want to write short stories because they're short, and by short, they mean short in every way. They think that a short story is an incomplete action in which a very little is shown and a great deal suggested, and they think you suggest something by leaving it out. It's very hard to disabuse a student of this notion, because he thinks that when he leaves something out, he's being subtle; and when you tell him that he has to put something in before anything can be there, he thinks you're an insensitive idiot.

Perhaps the central question to be considered in any discussion of the short story is what do we mean by short. Being short does not mean being slight. A short story should be long in depth and should give us an experience of meaning. I have an aunt who thinks that nothing happens in a story unless somebody gets married or shot at the end of it. I wrote a story about a tramp who marries an old woman's idiot daughter in order to acquire the old woman's automobile. After the marriage, he takes the daughter off on a wedding trip in the automobile and abandons her in an eating place and drives on by himself. Now that is a complete story. There is nothing more relating to the mystery of that man's personality that could be shown through that particular dramatization. But I've never been able to convince my aunt that it's a complete story. She wants to know what happened to the idiot daughter after that.

Not long ago that story was adapted for a television play, and the adapter, knowing his business, had the tramp have a change of heart and go back and pick up the idiot daughter and the two of them ride away, grinning madly. My aunt believes that the story is complete at last, but I have other sentiments about it—which are not suitable for public utterance. When you write a story, you only have to write one story, but there will always be people who will refuse to read the story you have written.

And this naturally brings up the awful question of what kind of a reader you are writing for when you write fiction. Perhaps we each think we have a personal solution for this problem. For my own part, I have a very high opinion of the art of fiction and a very low opinion of what is called the "average" reader. I tell myself that I can't escape him, that this is the personality I am supposed to keep awake, but that at the same time, I am also supposed to provide the intelligent reader with the deeper experience that he looks for in fiction. Now actually, both of these readers are just aspects of the writer's own personality, and in the last analysis, the only reader he can know anything about is himself. We all write at our own level of understanding, but it is the peculiar characteristic of fiction that its literal surface can be made to yield entertainment on an obvious physical plane to one sort of reader while the selfsame surface can be made to yield meaning to the person equipped to experience it there.

Meaning is what keeps the short story from being short. I prefer to talk about the meaning in a story rather than the theme of a story. People talk about the theme of a story as if the theme were like the string that a sack of chicken feed is tied with. They think that if you can pick out the theme, the way you pick the right thread in the chicken-feed sack, you can rip the story open and feed the chickens. But this is not the way meaning works in fiction.

When you can state the theme of a story, when you can separate it from the story itself, then you can be sure the story is not a very good one. The meaning of a story has to be embodied in it, has to be made concrete in it. A story is a way to say something that can't be said any other way, and it takes every word in the story to say what the meaning is. You tell a story because a statement would be inadequate. When anybody asks what a story is about, the only proper thing is to tell him to read the story. The meaning of fiction is not abstract meaning but experienced meaning, and the purpose of making statements about the meaning of a story is only to help you to experience that meaning more fully.

Fiction is an art that calls for the strictest attention to the real—whether the writer is writing a naturalistic story or a fantasy. I mean that we always begin with what is or with what has an eminent possibility of truth about it. Even when one writes a fantasy, reality is the proper basis of it. A thing is fantastic because it is so real, so real that it is fantastic. Graham Greene has said that he can't write, "I stood over a bottomless pit," because that couldn't be true, or "Running down the stairs I jumped into a taxi," because that couldn't be true either. But Elizabeth Bowen can write about one of her characters that "she snatched at her hair as if she heard something in it," because that is eminently possible.

I would even go so far as to say that the person writing a fantasy has to be even more strictly attentive to the concrete detail than someone writing in a naturalistic vein—because the greater the story's strain on the credulity, the more convincing the properties in it have to be.

A good example of this is a story called "The Metamorphosis" by Franz Kafka. This is a story about a man who wakes up one morning to find that he has turned into a cockroach overnight, while not discarding his human nature. The rest of the story concerns his life and feelings and eventual death as an insect with human nature, and this situation is accepted by the reader because the concrete detail of the story is absolutely convincing. The fact is that this story describes the dual nature of man in such a realistic fashion that it is almost unbearable. The truth is not distorted here, but rather, a certain distortion is used to get at the truth. If we admit, as we must, that appearance is not the same thing as reality, then we must give the artist the liberty to make certain rearrangements of nature if these will lead to greater depths of vision. The artist himself always has to remember that what he is rearranging *is* nature, and that he has to know it and be able to describe it accurately in order to have the authority to rearrange it at all.

The peculiar problem of the short-story writer is how to make the action he describes reveal as much of the mystery of existence as possible. He has only a short space to do it in and he can't do it by statement. He has to do it by showing, not by saying, and by showing the concrete—so that his problem is really how to make the concrete work double time for him.

In good fiction, certain of the details will tend to accumulate meaning from the action of the story itself, and when this happens they become symbolic in the way they work. I once wrote a story called "Good Country People," in which a lady Ph.D. has her wooden leg stolen by a Bible salesman whom she has tried to seduce. Now I'll admit that, paraphrased in this way, the situation is simply a low joke. The average reader is pleased to observe anybody's wooden leg being stolen. But without ceasing to appeal to him and without making any statements of high intention, this story does manage to operate at another level of experience, by letting the wooden leg accumulate meaning. Early in the story, we're presented with the fact that the Ph.D. is spiritually as well as physically crippled. She believes in nothing but her own belief in nothing, and we perceive that there is a wooden part of her soul that corresponds to her wooden leg. Now of course this is never stated. The fiction writer states as little as possible. The reader makes this connection from things he is shown. He may not even know that he makes the connection, but the connection is there nevertheless and it has its effect on him. As the story goes on, the wooden leg continues to accumulate meaning. The reader learns how the girl feels about her leg, how her mother feels about it, and how the country woman on the place feels about it; and finally, by the time the Bible salesman comes along, the leg has accumulated so much meaning that it is, as the saying goes, loaded. And when the Bible salesman steals it, the reader realizes that he has taken away part of the girl's personality and has revealed her deeper affliction to her for the first time.

If you want to say that the wooden leg is a symbol, you can say that. But it is a wooden leg first, and as a wooden leg it is absolutely necessary to the story. It has its place on the literal level of the story, but it operates in depth as well as on the surface. It increases the story in every direction, and this is essentially the way a story escapes being short.

Now a little might be said about the way in which this happens. I wouldn't want you to think that in that story I sat down and said, "I am now going to write a story about a Ph.D. with a wooden leg, using the wooden leg as a symbol for another kind of affliction." I doubt myself if many writers know what they are going to do when they start out. When I started writing that story, I didn't know there was going to be a Ph.D. with a wooden leg in it. I merely found myself one morning writing a description of two women that I knew something about, and before I realized it, I had equipped one of them with a daughter with a wooden leg. As the story progressed, I brought in the Bible salesman, but I had no idea what I was going to do with him. I didn't know he was going to steal that wooden leg until ten or twelve lines before he did it, but when I found out that this was what was going to happen, I realized that it was inevitable. This is a story that produces a shock for the reader, and I think one reason for this is that it produced a shock for the writer.

Now despite the fact that this story came about in this seemingly mind-less fashion, it is a story that almost no rewriting was done on. It is a story that was under control throughout the writing of it, and it might be asked how this kind of control comes about, since it is not entirely conscious.

I think the answer to this is what Maritain calls "the habit of art." It is a fact that fiction writing is something in which the whole personality takes part—the conscious as well as the unconscious mind. Art is the habit of the artist; and habits have to be rooted deep in the whole personality. They have to be cultivated like any other habit, over a long period of time, by experience; and teaching any kind of writing is largely a matter of helping the student develop the habit of art. I think this is more than just a discipline, although it is that; I think it is a way of looking at the created world and of using the senses so as to make them find as much meaning as possible in things.

Now I am not so naïve as to suppose that most people come to writers' conferences in order to hear what kind of vision is necessary to write stories that will become a permanent part of our literature. Even if you do wish to hear this, your greatest concerns are immediately practical. You want to know how you can actually write a good story, and further, how you can tell when you've done it; and so you want to know what the form of a short story is, as if the form were something that existed outside of each story and could be applied or imposed on the material. Of course, the more you write, the more you will realize that the form is organic, that it is something that grows out of the material, that the form of each story is unique. A story that is any good can't be reduced, it can only be expanded. A story is good when you continue to see more and more in it, and when it continues to escape you. In fiction two and two is always more than four.

The only way, I think, to learn to write short stories is to write them, and then to try to discover what you have done. The time to think of technique is when you've actually got the story in front of you. The teacher can help the student by looking at his individual work and trying to help him decide if he has written a complete story, one in which the action fully illuminates the meaning.

Perhaps the most profitable thing I can do is to tell you about some of the general observations I made about these seven stories I read of yours. All of these observations will not fit any one of the stories exactly, but they are points nevertheless that it won't hurt anyone interested in writing to think about.

The first thing that any professional writer is conscious of in reading anything is, naturally, the use of language. Now the use of language in these stories was such that, with one exception, it would be difficult to distinguish one story from another. While I can recall running into several clichés, I can't remember one image or one metaphor from the seven stories. I don't mean there weren't images in them; I just mean that there weren't any that were effective enough to take away with you.

In connection with this, I made another observation that startled me considerably. With the exception of one story, there was practically no use made of the local idiom. Now this is a Southern Writers' Conference. All the addresses on these stories were from Georgia or Tennessee, yet there was no distinctive sense of Southern life in them. A few place-names were dropped, Savannah or Atlanta or Jacksonville, but these could just as easily have been changed to Pittsburgh or Passaic without calling for any other alteration in the story. The characters spoke as if they had never heard any kind of language except what came out of a television set. This indicates that something is way out of focus.

There are two qualities that make fiction. One is the sense of mystery and the other is the sense of manners. You get the manners from the texture of existence that surrounds you. The great advantage of being a Southern writer is that we don't have to go anywhere to look for manners; bad or good, we've got them in abundance. We in the South live in a society that is rich in contradiction, rich in irony, rich in contrast, and particularly rich in its speech. And yet here are six stories by Southerners in which almost no use is made of the gifts of the region.

Of course the reason for this may be that you have seen these gifts abused so often that you have become self-conscious about using them. There is nothing worse than the writer who doesn't *use* the gifts of the region, but wallows in them. Everything becomes so Southern that it's sickening, so local that it is unintelligible, so literally reproduced that it conveys nothing. The general gets lost in the particular instead of being shown through it.

However, when the life that actually surrounds us is totally ignored, when our patterns of speech are absolutely overlooked, then something is out of kilter. The writer should then ask himself if he is not reaching out for a kind of life that is artificial to him.

An idiom characterizes a society, and when you ignore the idiom, you are very likely ignoring the whole social fabric that could make a meaningful character. You can't cut characters off from their society and say much about them as individuals. You can't say anything meaningful about the mystery of a personality unless you put that personality in a believable and significant social context. And the best way to do this is through the character's own language. When the old lady in one of Andrew Lytle's stories says contemptuously that she has a mule that is older than Birmingham, we get in that one sentence a sense of a society and its history. A great deal of the Southern writer's work is done for him before he begins, because our history lives in our talk. In one of Eudora Welty's stories a character says, "Where I come from, we use fox for yard dogs and owls for chickens, but we sing true." Now there is a whole book in that one sentence; and when the people of your section can talk like that, and you ignore it, you're just not taking advantage of what's yours. The sound of our talk is too definite to be discarded with impunity, and if the writer tries to get rid of it, he is liable to destroy the better part of his creative power.

Another thing I observed about these stories is that most of them don't go very far inside a character, don't reveal very much of the character. I don't mean that they don't enter the character's mind, but they simply don't show that he has a personality. Again this goes back partly to speech. These characters have no distinctive speech to reveal themselves with; and sometimes they have no really distinctive features. You feel in the end that no personality is revealed because no personality is there. In most good stories it is the character's personality that creates the action of the story. In most of these stories, I feel that the writer has thought of some action and then scrounged up a character to perform it. You will usually be more successful if you start the other way around. If you start with a real personality, a real character, then something is bound to happen; and you don't have to know what before you begin. In fact it may be better if you don't know what before you begin. You ought to be able to discover something from your stories. If you don't, probably nobody else will.

Donald Hall attended Harvard, Oxford, and Stanford. After years of teaching at the University of Michigan, Goddard College, and elsewhere, Hall wrote a series of best-selling textbooks and college anthologies that freed him to devote full time to his poetry. Hall admits that he sometimes takes up to four years to complete a poem, yet since 1955 he has published and edited more than twenty-five books, the most recent being *Kicking the Leaves* (1978), *Remembering Poets* (1978), *Goatfoot, Milktongue, Twinbird* (1978), and *The Oxcart Man* (1979), a children's book that won the Caldecott Medal. He has also won the Lamont Poetry Award and two Guggenheim Fellowships. Hall currently serves as General Editor of the University of Michigan Poets on Poetry Series. "I work hard," he says, "but most of all I believe in endurance and courage."

Writing Poems

Donald Hall

If we love poetry, we usually try to write it. I think that an excellent way to learn to read poems is to try to write them. (Creative writing courses can be justified only on these grounds; we cannot turn out poets as if we were General Motors turning out cars.) Mostly, we learn by writing what we want to write, and then by being tough on ourselves, and crossing out, and rewriting and rewriting. Writing is extremely hard work. Practically no one has ever found it easy, or has been able to write decently on a first draft. But writing poetry is an enormous pleasure. Once a man has had the pleasure of making a metaphor. . . .

The attitude to cultivate from the start is that revision is a way of life. We must write the first time as well as we can; then stare at it until we can see holes in it, cross out, write in what we can, and then cross out some more. So what if it takes us a long time to write a poem? What are we living for anyway?

Poets learn craft by revision, but they cannot tinker with the essentially mediocre and make it great. Some poets believe in throwing away their un-successful drafts and starting again. A poet I know has told me that some-times, when a poem is not coming right, he will take a nap and then write a new draft immediately on waking, without reference to the old version. We

Source: *"Writing Poems," from* The Pleasure of Poetry *by Donald Hall. Copyright © 1971 by Donald Hall. Reprinted by permission of Harper & Row, Publishers, Inc.*

all have to find our own ways. Sometimes when I was writing formal poems I could make a form come right by switching the form, like changing pentameter quatrains into tetrameter couplets. (Rhyming "The Sleeping Giant" seemed to help the poem.) I remember the advice Auguste Rodin gave young sculptors when they were having trouble with a maquette (a model, in wax or clay or whatever, of a big sculpture). He told them not to keep poking it with tools and making minor changes, but to drop it on the floor and see what it looked like then.

Some people—deliberately or not—have learned by imitation. I think it is typical, in fact, when we are young to learn by a series of infatuations. This month I imitate Yeats, next week Marvell, next month Roethke. Each time I learn something new. Some artists have set out purposely to imitate styles and have learned to extend their own abilities. As in athletics or in acting, we can learn by mimickry. Eventually, when we are at the right point, we assert our own identity. But there is no pushing it. It comes or it doesn't come.

Getting ideas is the hard part. It seems to me that I have to wait on them. But a lighter, or imitative, kind of poem—a practice poem—can be fabricated. We can also fabricate a wild surrealism, writing "automatically" and deliberately not knowing what we are doing. Some artists have suppressed their rationality by drugs or alcohol, others by techniques of meditation. I know a young poet who made a breakthrough by writing with earphones blasting rock music into his head.

In time we develop a nose for poems. In the beginning, I would advise against trying to write about big abstractions, like "Love" or "Racial Conflict." We should write instead about a tree or a person, and let our feelings come through the images we use. In fact, the best way to begin writing poems is to begin with descriptions. Ideas and feelings come in, as we describe. When we start from the Big Idea, we write with the substance of a cloud. "Love" is a word with no love in it. "Cool thighs," "long hair"—these are phrases that might begin to contain love, or erotic feeling.

So, as Ezra Pound said a long time ago, "Go in fear of abstractions." If we can write a poem without any of them, *just* using touch/feel/see/hear/smell words, chances are we will write more movingly.

Also, go in fear of clichés and dead metaphors. We develop a sense of tact that identifies them, and cut them out. Everybody writes them in first drafts; that is why first drafts won't do. It takes a while, and usually the eyes of other readers, to get rid of all the commonplace language our heads are stuffed with. Reading our poems literally (can a door both "yawn" and "beckon"?) will help.

With rhythm, advice gets harder. Mere meter can be counted, but to make good noises seems like an instinctive thing. If it is not instinctive, it is based on reading hundreds and thousands of poems, and on revising our own over and over again. This is the kind of knowledge which we learn in order to forget—the tennis stroke, or riding a bicycle—and it is obviously acquired knowledge, but it comes to seem instinctual. Our sense of the form of the poem—that click of the box which is a resolution of rhythm, image, and feeling—lies deep inside us, but it comes from our reading, in which we develop our changing sense of what a good poem is, and from our revising toward that goal.

One or two things, at least, can be said about a rhythm. Short-lined free verse which stops the sense at the end of a line sounds prosy:

> *It has no interest*
> *because the sense*
> *is the same as the line.*
> *There is no difference.*
> *One can go on and on*
> *chopping prose like this.*

So short-lined free verse usually needs enjambment, and long-lined free verse does not, though it can tolerate it. One cannot generalize about iambic pentameter, except to say that counting it and having it come out right is not enough. Iambic pentameter can work well either end-stopped or enjambed. When we use a shorter line, like a dimeter or a trimeter, the same rule of thumb applies which applied to free verse: better run-on.

The language of our poems must grow from the way we talk. A student of mine once wrote in a poem that he went into "the Romance Languages Building every morn." Until the last word he was talking his own language; then he was talking book talk. The trouble with archaic language is very much like the trouble with clichés: It puts a barrier between the reader and the feeling, a barrier of old books, or, in the case of clichés, a barrier of newspapers or slovenly speech. The only true test for idiomatic diction, when we are interrogating our drafts, looking for things to cut out, is: Could I conceivably have spoken these words without irony? My student would never have said to his roommate that he was off to the Romance Language Building this morn.

Maybe one of the most important things to have, when we are writing poems, is a reader. The reader must be an embodied Muse, someone sympathetic to our endeavors, but hard on us—someone to point out clichés, dead metaphors, rhythmical ineptitude, archaisms, and other mistakes.

A final technical matter—small but important—is the adjective. Virtually every beginning poet hurts himself by an addiction to adjectives. Verbs are by far the most important things for poems—especially wonderful tough monosyllables like "grasp" and "cry." Nouns are the next most important. Adjectives tend to be useless. The right one at the right time is perfect, but the typical amateur writes with every noun carrying its little adjective, like a puny bodyguard. "The white snow on the green grass is like. . . ." "Snow on grass" is stronger and quicker.

Compression is an important thing, and omitting adjectives can often compress and strengthen at the same time, "Grass" is a bit greener than "green grass"; it is surely shorter. Also, in a poem where three images are doing the same thing, it is stronger to omit two and keep one. Less is more. That slogan is one to bear in mind.

Most of us tend to overexplain. From a lack of confidence in our images, we add a useless line or stanza of editorial comment, usually a nudge-in-the-ribs which says, "in case you didn't get it, this is what I meant," and makes an abstract summary of content. But abstract summaries tend to weaken the real emotion of images and metaphors. Abstractions often limit the ambivalent range of feeling which concrete words are able to carry. Once I wrote a poem in which I embodied feelings of being stuck and paralyzed by describing a skeleton strapped in the cockpit of an undiscovered, crashed, World War II fighter plane. At the end I said that even if the pilot had made it back to the aircraft carrier, and was alive now, he would feel the same way:

> *. . . and every*
> *morning takes his chair, his pale*
> *hands on the black arms, and sits*
> *upright, held*
> *by the firm webbing.*

As it ends now, I hope everyone can recognize the feeling, which all of us undergo from time to time. But when I first wrote the poem, I overexplained: ". . . the firm webbing/of job and house and. . . ." By my overspecificity, I limited the feeling to a man with a job and a house. The feeling of being stuck belongs to everybody—high school students, old people, housewives—it is not my property alone.

Finally, of course, poetry is not a matter of slogans but of the spirit. We must learn—if we are to write well—to discover the dark parts of ourselves and be true to them. We must also learn the shapes and feelings of words in the mouth, and what feels best. We must learn to make art. Art is long and life is short.

But however long we work, and however much or little public success comes to us, we will never arrive anywhere. If we feel that we know we are good, we are already dead—like the skeleton in the cockpit. When I was young I thought that we climbed a mountain to reach a plateau. Now I know that we climb to climb, and if we ever reach a place where we can see no rocks above us, we have fallen down the mountain. Old poets give us examples of this continuing labor. The greatest influence old poets can have on contemporary ones is spiritual and not stylistic. I always think of Yeats, who revised his poems continually, and who throughout his life expressed his dissatisfaction with what he had written in the past. In poems and in letters we see him continually disappointed in what he has accomplished but determined to continue trying. Shortly before he died he wrote the poem, "The Circus Animal's Desertion," in which he dismissed his life's work, but swore at the end, "I must lie down where all the ladders start,/In the foul rag-and-bone shop of the heart." Three weeks before he died he wrote a letter saying that he was resting, "after writing much verse." He knows "for certain that my time will not be long..." but, "In two or three weeks ... I will begin to write my most fundamental thoughts...."

To die like that, in the midst of work, is the best death anyone could wish for. In writing poems, as in everything else, the work is the thing and not the response to the work. Though we may work for potential love or fame, applause for our old work is nothing if we are not making new poems. When we are not in the midst of working, applause is almost a curse; it is a reminder that we are no longer the person who did the old work. Whether we are Nobel prize winners or unrecognized beginners, the pleasure of writing poetry is one-fiftieth in the praise, and the rest in the act of making a metaphor.

Suggested Readings

The following bibliography includes a wide range of theoretical studies, autobiographies, biographies, and essays. We have not limited our selection only to writers because we have found that artists, scientists, psychologists, and others have all made significant contributions to the study of the creative process.

Anderson, Sherwood. *A Story Teller's Story*. Edited by Ray Lewis White. Cleveland: The Press of Case Western Reserve University, 1968.

Arieti, Silvano. *Creativity: The Magic Synthesis*. New York: Basic Books, 1976.

Barlow, J. E. "Long Day's Journey Into Night: From Early Notes to Finished Play." *Modern Drama*, 22 (March 1979), 19–28.

Bogan, Louise. *Journey Around My Room*. New York: Viking Press, 1980.

Brande, Dorothea. *Becoming a Writer*. Los Angeles: J. P. Tarcher, 1981.

Burnshaw, Stanley. *The Seamless Web*. New York: George Braziller, 1970.

Cary, Joyce. *Art and Reality: Ways of the Creative Process*. New York: Harper, 1958.

Cowley, Malcolm. "How Writers Write" in *And I Worked at the Writer's Trade*. Viking Press: New York, 1978.

Didion, Joan. "Why I Write." *New York Times Book Review*, December 5, 1976, p. 2.

Doggett, F. "Stevens on the Genesis of A Poem." *Contemporary Literature*, 16 (Autumn 1975), 463–77.

Edwards, Betty. *Drawing on the Right Side of The Brain*. Los Angeles: J. P. Tarcher, 1979.

Edwards, Don, and Carol Polsgrove. "A Conversation with John Gardner." *The Atlantic Monthly*, May, 1977, pp. 43–47.

Eiseley, Loren. *All the Strange Hours*. New York: Scribner's, 1975.

———. *The Night Country*. New York: Charles Scribner's Sons, 1971.

Elbow, Peter. *Writing Without Teachers*. London: Oxford University Press, 1973.

Ghiselin, Brewster, ed. *The Creative Process*. New York: New American Library, 1958.

Gibbons, Reginald, ed. *The Poet's Work: 29 Masters of 20th Century Poetry on the Origins and Practice of their Art*. Boston: Houghton Mifflin Co., 1979.

Gilder, Joshua. "Creators on Creating: Tom Wolfe." *Saturday Review*, April, 1981, pp. 40–44.

Givner, J. "Her Great Art, Her Sober Craft: Katherine Anne Porter's Creative Process." *Southwest Review* 62 (Summer 1977), 217–30.

Hall, Donald. *Goatfoot, Milktongue, Twinbird*. Ann Arbor, Michigan: University of Michigan Press, 1978.

Hawkes, John. "Notes on Writing a Novel." *Tri Quarterly* 30 (Spring 1974): 109–26.

Heyen, William, ed. *American Poets in 1976*. Indianapolis: Bobbs-Merrill, 1977.

Horgan, Paul. *Approaches to Writing*. New York: Farrar, Straus and Giroux, 1973.

Hugo, Richard. *The Triggering Town: Lectures on Poetry and Writing*. New York: W. W. Norton, 1979.

Ignatow, David. *Open Between Us*. Ann Arbor: University of Michigan Press, 1980.

Jacob, Max. *Advice to a Young Poet*. Translated by John Adlard. London: Menard Press, 1976.

Jong, Erica. "Writing a First Novel." *Twentieth Century Literature* 20 (October 1974): 262–69.

Kinnell, Galway. *Walking Down the Stairs: Selections from Interviews*. Ann Arbor: University of Michigan Press, 1978.

Krutch, Joseph Wood. *Experience and Art*. New York: Collier, 1962.

Kuehl, John, ed. *Creative Writing and Rewriting: Contemporary American Novelists at Work*. New York: Appleton-Century-Crofts, 1967.

Kunitz, Stanley. *A Kind of Order, A Kind of Folly*. Boston: Little, Brown, 1975.

Le Guin, Ursula. *The Language of the Night: Essays on Fantasy and Science Fiction*. Edited by Susan Wood. New York: G. P. Putnam's Sons, 1979.

Levertov, Denise. *The Poet in the World.* New York: New Directions, 1973.

Mansfield, Katherine. *Journal of Katherine Mansfield.* Edited by J. Middleton Murry. New York: A. A. Knopf, 1927.

May, Rollo. *The Courage to Create.* New York: W. W. Norton, 1975.

Mills, Hilary. "Creators on Creating: E. L. Doctorow." *Saturday Review,* October, 1980, pp. 44–48.

————. "Creators on Creating: William Styron." *Saturday Review,* September, 1980, pp. 46–50.

Mills, Hilary. "Creators on Creating: Norman Mailer." *Saturday Review,* January, 1981, pp. 46–53.

Mills, Ralph Jr. *Cry of the Human.* Chicago: University of Illinois Press, 1975.

Morris, Wright. *About Fiction.* New York: Harper and Row, 1975.

————. *Conversations with Wright Morris.* Edited by Robert E. Knoll. Lincoln: University of Nebraska Press, 1977.

Nemerov, Howard. *Journal of a Fictive Life.* Brunswick, N.J.: Rutgers University Press, 1965.

————, ed. *Poets on Poetry.* New York: Basic Books, 1966.

Neruda, Pablo. *Memoirs.* New York: Farrar, Straus and Giroux, 1977.

Nin, Anaïs. *Diary of Anaïs Nin,* 7 vols. New York: Harcourt Brace Jovanovich, 1978.

————. *The Novel of the Future.* New York: Macmillan, 1968.

O'Connor, Flannery. *The Habit of Being.* Edited by Sally Fitzgerald. New York: Farrar, Straus and Giroux, 1980.

————. *Mystery and Manners: Occasional Prose.* Edited by Robert and Sally Fitzgerald. New York: Farrar, Straus and Giroux, 1969.

O'Keeffe, Georgia. *Georgia O'Keeffe.* New York: Viking Press, 1976.

Olsen, Tillie. *Silences.* New York: Delacorte Press/Seymour Lawrence, 1978.

Plimpton, George, ed. *Writers at Work: The Paris Review Interviews.* New York: Viking Press, 1958, 1963, 1967, 1976.

Pollitt, Katha. "Creators on Creating: Isaac Bashevis Singer." *Saturday Review,* July, 1980, pp. 46–50.

————. "Creators on Creating: Bernard Malamud." *Saturday Review,* February, 1981, pp. 32–39.

Rich, Adrienne. "When We Dead Awaken: Writing as Re-vision." *College English* 34 (October 1972): 18–25.

Rilke, Rainer Maria. *Letters to A Young Poet.* Translated by M. D. Herter Norton. New York: W. W. Norton, 1963.

Roethke, Theodore. *On the Poet and His Craft.* Edited by Ralph J. Mills, Jr. Seattle, Washington: University of Washington Press, 1965.

_____. *Straw for the Fire*. Selected and arranged by David Wagoner. Garden City, N.Y.: Doubleday, 1972.

Rosner, Stanley, and Lawrence E. Abts, eds. *The Creative Experience*. New York: Grossman, 1970.

Rubinstein, Leonard. *Writing: A Habit of Mind*. Dubuque, Iowa: Wm. C. Brown Co., 1972.

Sagan, Carl. *Dragons of Eden*. New York: Random House, 1977.

Sarton, May. *Journal of Solitude*. New York: W. W. Norton, 1973.

Seager, Allan. *The Glass House*. New York: McGraw-Hill, 1968.

Seferis, George. *A Poet's Journal: Days of 1945–1951*. Harvard University Press, 1974.

Spender, Stephen. *The Making of a Poem*. Westport, Conn.: Greenwood Press, 1976.

Stafford, William. "Attempts That Became Poems: Some Journal Scribblings and Revisions Toward Print." *Northwest Review*, 13 (1973), 10–20.

_____. *Writing the Australian Crawl: Views on the Writer's Vocation*. Ann Arbor: The University of Michigan Press, 1978.

Steinbeck, John. *Journal of A Novel: The East of Eden Letters*. New York: Viking Press, 1969.

Stewart, Donald C. *The Authentic Voice*. Dubuque, Iowa: Wm. C. Brown Co., 1972.

"Symposium: The Writer's Situation" in *New American Review*, April, 1970, pp. 61–100.

Thornley, Wilson R. *Short Story Writing*. 3rd ed. New York: Bantam, 1979.

Tucker, Carl. "Creators on Creating: Henry Moore." *Saturday Review*, March, 1981, pp. 42–46.

Turner, Alberta T. *Fifty Contemporary Poets: The Creative Process*. New York: McKay, 1977.

Van Gogh, Vincent. *Dear Theo: The Autobiography of Vincent Van Gogh*. Edited by Irving Stone. New York: New American Library, 1969.

Wagoner, Linda Welshimer. *The Poems of William Carlos Williams*. Middletown, Conn.: Wesleyan Press, 1963.

Webber, Jeannette L. and Joan Grumman eds. *Woman as Writer*. Boston: Houghton Mifflin, 1978.

Welty, Eudora. *The Eye of the Story*. New York: Random House, 1978.

West, William W. *On Writing, By Writers*. Boston: Ginn and Co., 1966.

Wilbur, Richard. *Responses: Prose Pieces 1948–1974*. New York: Harcourt Brace Jovanovich, 1976.

_____. "The Problem of Creative Thinking in Poetry." *In the Writer's Mind*.

Edited by Wallace Kaufman and William Powers. Englewood Cliffs, N.J.: Prentice-Hall, 1970.

Williams, William Carlos. *I Wanted to Write a Poem.* Reported and edited by Edith Heal. Boston: Beacon Press, 1958.

Woolf, Virginia. *A Room of One's Own.* New York: Harcourt Brace Jovanovich, 1929.

———. *A Writer's Diary.* Edited by Leonard Woolf. New York: Harcourt Brace Jovanovich, 1954.

Wright, Judith. *Because I Was Invited.* Melbourne: Oxford University Press, 1975.